love
you
bye

love
you
bye

A Memoir

Rossandra White

SHE WRITES PRESS

Published 2014
Printed in the United States of America
ISBN: 978-1-938314-50-6
Library of Congress Control Number: 2013953913

For information, address:
She Writes Press
1563 Solano Ave #546
Berkeley, CA 94707

For my brother Garth and to

the memory of Sweetpea

"Life must be understood backwards, [Although] . . . it must be lived forwards" —Soren Kierkegaard.

one

IT WAS DAWN when I headed down from our loft bedroom, down steep, narrow steps that wouldn't have been out of place in a submarine, except that these didn't have any banisters. As always, I mostly skipped down those steps. In the old days my husband, Larry, would take the steps one at a time, crab-like.

That's when he used to sleep with me. This was before he retired. One thing and another, and he started spending more and more nights downstairs on our Southwestern-hued sectional, which had become his bed. There was nowhere else to sleep in our tiny house. He made half-assed excuses about how it had become too hot upstairs, too crowded in bed with our dogs, Sweetpea and Jake, and how the staircase, all of a sudden, was too dangerous to negotiate in the middle of the night when he had to pee. He was the one who built it, along with my youngest son, Layne, and a couple of cases of beer—he was the one responsible for its rail-less state. This was no big deal in the beginning, and by the time it mattered to him, he was sick of working on the house.

I dressed quickly for work in the room below, a kind of dressing room cum office, using the closet light to see in case Larry had fallen back asleep next door on the sectional after letting the dogs out to do their business. The light went on in the kitchen, followed by the thud of the refrigerator door. I grinned. I liked it when he got up with me in the morning. It didn't often happen. It usually meant fresh squeezed orange juice. And his company. Maybe an improvement in his attitude.

By the time I'd brushed my teeth and slapped on makeup, he was perched on the ratty footstool in the kitchen, the newspaper between his hands. He wore his usual shorts, surf sweatshirt, and flip-flops. Sweetpea and Jake, Staffordshire Bull Terriers—picture a cross between a pot-bellied pig and the cartoon warthog from *The Lion King*—were doing their rabid dog charge through the dining room and kitchen. An overturned dog food bowl and scattered kibble lay in their wake. Larry grinned at their antics. A glass of orange juice stood on the counter.

"Thanks," I said.

"You're welcome," he said in that warm drawl of his without looking up. I took a swig of orange juice, turned on the kettle, and then reached into the cupboard for my cup and threw in a tea bag.

Sweetpea ambled over and sat on my foot. I bent down, grabbed her ears and kissed her between the eyes. Jake charged over; I kissed the top of his head and straightened.

"Surfing, today?" I glanced at the clock. "Shit, I'm going to be late."

"You're always late."

Ten minutes later, my African straw bag crammed with an assortment of the must-have items I ferried to and from work—the Great African novel I was working on, my vitamin pill box, running shoes, a book, extra batteries for my music at work—I stopped in front of Larry. I knew better, but I hoped for a good-bye peck. He glanced up, his slate-blue eyes clear and open.

"Have a good day," he said, pleasantly, making no move toward me.

Why did I keep setting myself up like that? I could bend down and kiss him, but his half-hearted response would remind me once again how distant he'd become and then I'd be pissed at myself for trying. Well, at least there was the orange juice. That had to mean something.

"You too," I said, heading for the door with Sweetpea and Jake close behind.

Larry's note lay on the kitchen counter when I got home from work: "Gone to Mexico. Adios."

This couldn't be happening again. I smoothed the small, hot pink notepaper meant for quickie grocery lists. My fingers shook. His neat little boy handwriting—letters so small and meticulous—so unlike his laid-back attitude—made the words seem ordinary, like he'd checked with me, like I'd agreed. Just like the other three notes he'd left on the kitchen counter over the past eight months, same cryptic message with a few changes in the wording, always Mexico, always on the same multicolored notepad. Those trips had lasted anywhere from a week to ten days. I'd thought that after his last escape two months earlier, that would be it; he'd get back on track, maybe finally let me know what had been bothering him.

It suddenly struck me that our 1988 white VW was missing from its usual spot beside his 1973 green Chevy van in the vacant lot next to the house. He'd been driving the smaller car ever since he started working on the van's engine two months earlier. I hadn't even noticed. So would he be sleeping in the VW?

Or had he finally taken that surfer pal's offer to stay at his Ensenada beach house? The guy had been inviting him for years; surfers down at his favorite spot in San Clemente were always inviting him on surf trips. They just wanted to hang with him. Everybody wanted to hang with him. He never went. He hated staying with other people, hated to be obligated to anyone.

After the shock of his first unexpected departure, I started thinking that maybe that's exactly what he needed, time alone on a surfboard down Mexico way. Out in the ocean, catching waves, with that occasional brush with a dolphin he treasured so much—this was where he found his spiritual center. Maybe he'd finally grieve the loss of his mother. She died right before he retired, which was when he planned on spending more time with her. I knew that was a big deal for him. He felt guilty. Not that he said anything about it. No signs of grief, even at the funeral—well, except for convulsively squeezing my hand. The shrink told me he was probably depressed and advised lots of loving understanding. As far as our seeking counseling together, Larry told me I had the problem, not him.

I thought back to our confrontation after his last defection, two months earlier. Not that much different from the other times.

"Okay, so are you finally going to tell me what's going on?"

"What do you mean?"

"Why do you keep doing this?"

"Doing what?"

We went back and forth like this for a bit, with me becoming more and more agitated because of his stonewalling. This, of course, just made him calmer and me crazier until I stormed off. This was how most of our confrontations went. But then he'd come through with a self-effacing sweetness and life would continue.

I glanced at the note. "Adios." I felt my jaw tighten.

Sweetpea and Jake slammed against the back of my legs, vying for my attention. I glanced down. Almond-shaped eyes with white half-moons stared up at me with devoted Staffie intensity. I dropped to my knees, grabbed them both around the neck and squeezed hard.

They yelped and wriggled free then spun back around and licked my face, all the while bumping and grinding against each other. In a wild Tasmanian devil whirl of scrapping, they disappeared around the corner. I flopped on the floor, let my head fall back against the kitchen cabinets, and glanced around at the house I'd shared for twenty-five years with a man I thought I knew. So much for that.

"Hobbit House" is what my mother-in-law called our one-bedroom beach cottage. It had been cobbled together sometime around 1915. Larry had been the one to see its potential when we first looked at it. I didn't voice my doubts. All I'd ever known were the soulless, company-owned brick houses with corrugated tin roofs back in Nkana, Zambia, the dinky copper mining town in the middle of the African bush where I was raised, and the soulless tract house in Huntington Beach where I lived with my first husband.

It didn't take long for me to love our Hobbit house, especially since it was only a mile from the center of Laguna Beach, a quaint artists' colony. Its river rock fireplace and claw-foot bathtub were also part of its charm. Over the years we replaced the louvered windows with hand-crafted leaded glass, added oak floors, and cultivated a bamboo-enclosed paradise filled with begonias, staghorn ferns, bromeliads, succulents, and papyrus, along with a rock-encircled Koi pond.

"Winchester House" is what Larry's three sisters called the place, referring to the world-famous Winchester Mystery House in San Jose, an extravagant maze of Victorian craftsmanship continuously under construction for thirty-eight years, from 1884 until 1922. Larry had only been at it for twenty-five years, adding the loft and staircase, a dining room and studio. He'd had some help along the way from my youngest son, Layne. Unfortunately, their faulty measuring left inch-high ledges between the rooms, which became the cause of many a stubbed toe. Larry had also refurbished the bathroom, but seventeen years later had yet to re-hang the doors. This made for much teasing and speculation from family and friends as to our modesty, not to mention our sanity. I loved it. This was who I'd always secretly been, who we were together. A good fit.

I rose to my feet and headed for my office cum dressing room. I had to get out of here. Dressed in shorts, T-shirt, and running shoes, I headed for the utility room where I kept the dogs' collars and leashes. They trotted after me. They knew the drill.

Within minutes the three of us were walking down our rustic dead -end street toward Laguna Canyon Road and the beach, the dogs trailing their leashes. I had to pass Larry's green van, dubbed the "Love Cage," parked in the vacant lot next door, a forlorn sight without the battered VW beside it. That van was where we first made love. It was our motel on wheels for a trip up to Northern California ten years earlier to reunite with his two youngest adult daughters, missing for seventeen years after his ex-wife kidnapped them. She'd taken off with the guy they'd hired to do construction on their house.

I started to jog. Jake shot past me, dragging Sweetpea along by her leash for the first fifty yards like he usually did before dropping it to pee against the fire hydrant at the corner of Canyon Acres and Laguna Canyon Road. I bent down to retrieve her leash and let Jake lead the way.

When I looked up again, I was halfway down the side street that ran parallel to Laguna Canyon Road, in front of a mobile home park that had seen the likes of Timothy Leary: twenty hodgepodge trailers nestled in a horseshoe-shaped lot sprinkled with trees. High above the park, multimillion-dollar homes gazed out to sea, as if trying to ignore the odd little enclave below. Lodged sideways in front of the park was that weird little trailer that looked more like a kid's playhouse.

This had been my first taste of Laguna Beach, back when the famous Sawdust Festival, a hundred yards further down, was a hippie artists' venue. I'd been in America for nine years by then, still married to my South African husband and with nine- and eleven-year-old sons. I'd ventured from my embattled marriage in Huntington Beach to this very trailer with a girlfriend to visit a man who taught meditation. Oh, how appealing that whole world of hippies, free love, and consciousness-raising had been to me. How open and accepting.

In those days, the trailer's yard consisted of a small, unadorned wedge of grass edged with brick on the trailer park side and a fence along the street. Now, Golden Angel's Trumpet blooms dangled over the weathered fence and white daisies filled a pink polka-dotted planter below the front window. In the middle of the yard, a single pumpkin the size of Venus blossomed between two battered Adirondack chairs. Behind them on the fence, a carved wooden sign, the kind seen outside some seaside restaurants, issued an invitation for Sunday Brunch: below, a smaller one spelled out the words "Horn Dog." So Laguna Beach.

I still couldn't get over the sideways thinking that went on in Laguna. So unlike Nkana, where Rhokana Corporation provided workers with housing, medical care, schooling, and a recreational club. Everything in Nkana was painted either white or green, and whitewashed rocks edged the driveways, lawns, and trees. So predictable. So contained. So boring. Lately, though, I found myself missing those rocks; I could rely on them to define things.

After a quick walk on the beach, I returned home. Jake trotted beside me; Sweetpea lagged along behind. I turned and eyed her anxiously for signs of distress, for evidence that her one kidney was failing. A habit. My baby girl. The dog who was supposed to save my marriage.

Two

I THOUGHT BACK to the day we got Sweetpea. Larry reluctantly agreed to accompany me on the seventy-mile trip to the breeder. This was right after he retired. "Why do we need another shitting machine?" he wanted to know, although he brightened when he learned I had my heart set on a Staffie. I'd grown up with the breed back home, and he had been tickled by the spunk of a relative's Staffie on our last visit. I was thinking that a dog might open him up a little. Truth was, I was the one who needed a dog, especially a Staffie: over-the-top passionate and sensitive. It had been a long, lonely year since Suki, my fifteen-year old mutt, died.

But it was just me standing at the edge of the wire enclosure looking down at the eight black-and-brindle Staffie pups charging around. Larry had been his usual outwardly warm and friendly self meeting the breeder and his wife, and he now stood off to one side talking to the man. Sweetpea caught my eye immediately. At four pounds to her siblings' beefy nine, she was the runt of the litter. But she stood out. I don't know whether it was the patch of golden brindle fur gleaming like a light above her heart-shaped face, or the chipper way she bounced around the pen on her tiny back bowlegs. She just seemed so happy to be alive. I laughed and clapped my hands like a little kid. Larry gave me one of his

Whoa! looks and rolled his eyes. Reaching into the pen, I scooped her up. She nuzzled into my neck in a cloud of sweet puppy breath.

"We'll take her," I cried.

I called her Sweetpea. I was soon to discover that the name couldn't have been more apt. As we walked toward the car, I shoved the sleeping puppy into Larry's arms.

"I'll drive."

He didn't argue. He settled back against the passenger seat, Sweetpea cradled against his chest like a baby bird. Her tiny snores filled the car. From the corner of my eye, I watched him tentatively stroke her.

"You're a funny little thing, aren't you?" he whispered.

He held her against his chest all the way home. That was easy, I thought, one marshmallow coming up. The sun was setting as we got out of the car.

"Quite the pisser, aren't you?" He lowered Sweetpea onto the grass in the vacant lot next to our house. There was a small damp patch on his sweatshirt.

"She really must've had to go," I said.

Turned out, it was more than that. Much more. A little puppy leakage can happen, the breeder told us when I called him. But the damp patches grew as Sweetpea grew.

The vet said it could be anything from a bladder infection to ectopic ureter, where the tubes carrying urine from the kidneys aren't connected to the bladder and the pee just drips out. He didn't offer a solution, just a vague reference to the possibility of experimental surgery at The University School of Veterinary Medicine in Davis. Meanwhile, he tried different remedies. He also suggested we return her to the breeder, citing a California puppy lemon law. She'd most likely be put down. That was unthinkable.

Sweetpea had gotten under my skin in a way I couldn't explain, in a way no other animal ever had. The way she picked up on my feelings: an empath; a best girlfriend. When Larry and I fought, not even real fights, she'd ease up from her donut doggy bed and sit there in front of us like a temple dog, the whites of her eyes showing, anxious and tense.

And Larry. That was a surprise. He told me he didn't care if she flooded our entire house with pee: she was family. Family. Ironic. This was a man who could take 'em or leave 'em, including his own kids, yet he even stopped surfing in the morning for months because he didn't want to leave her alone while I was at work. Here's the funniest part of his attachment to her: Sometimes, when he stretched out beside her on the floor, his head beside hers on her donut bed, she'd shift around to face the other way. She also growled at him one time when he stopped her for a kiss on her way upstairs to sleep with me. Just a low rumble. This was right after he started disappearing. But here's the thing: right from the beginning Larry, thought this kind of behavior was hilarious and endearing. Miss Personality. He said it made him love her even more. I loved that he felt this way. But even she couldn't keep him here.

I realized with a start that Sweetpea had disappeared from the vacant lot. As the sun slipped behind the hill across the canyon, I spun around and noticed her head sticking out from behind a tree stump. She was sniffing around like a truffle hound with a find. Stalling. Getting her back in the yard was always a bitch. If she had her way she would live in the vacant lot. All the better to be available on the off chance some random human would come along. Staffies have an inordinate thing about connecting with people; Sweetpea embarrassingly so, more than Jake. She'd wait until that speck down the street turned into a human, then she'd do a slow wiggle toward them, her entire body a welcoming sign, her white-rimmed Staffie eyes illuminated from within like one of those round-eyed children in velvet paintings from Mexico who tear at your heart. "It's you," her look said. "At last!"

"How about a Greenie?" I called. Sweetpea's head shot up at the mention of her and Jake's favorite treat. She considered me for a moment, as if trying to decide whether this was a real offer or a ploy to get her back into the yard.

"A GREENIE!" I yelled. "Hey?"

I didn't often use a Greenie as bait, she was too smart for that, but I was in a hurry to get back inside. I felt edgy. A nice hot bath would go down well. And, of course, at the back of my mind was the idea Larry might call. Damn him.

Jake was already at the gate, nose pressed into the wood; he always took me at my word. Sweetpea considered me for a moment longer, gave a couple more sniffs, then trotted toward me, all cocky and happy.

The phone rang as I stepped into the house. I ran to answer it.

"Mom?" a familiar voice crackled through the line. It was Layne, my youngest son, calling from South Africa. He'd emigrated there eight years earlier.

I relaxed. "Hey, little bubs."

"It's all sorted. We both got all three weeks off, and of course the kids will be off for the Christmas hols."

"Huh?"

"Christmas? With your favorite son and his beautiful wife and family?"

"Oh. Oh, yes." I sank into the desk chair. Oh, no. My trip back to South Africa in seven weeks. On top of everything. Who would take care of the dogs if Larry didn't come back?

"Are you okay?"

"I—I'm good, I was just out with the dogs."

"Well, then how about a whoo-ya?"

"Whoo-ya."

"That was quite underwhelming. Lucky I'm the secure son. Listen, I spoke to Uncle Garth. He sounded good, can't wait to see all of us."

Garth. My poor, sweet brother. I slid further down into the chair. "What else did he say?"

"Not much. You know him; he's fine, Margaret's fine, everything's fine," he finished, his American twang flattening to imitate my brother's thick South African one.

"He's not fine. He's got a heart condition and he lives nine stories up in a flat with a broken elevator. His situation makes me crazy."

"Well, you'll be pleased to hear he's got another place lined up. The Somerset Hotel. Some kind of deal where they rent a couple of rooms to the handicapped at a reduced rate. I checked out the place on the web. Looks pretty nice."

"Wow!" I sat up. "That's amazing. I didn't know we had that kind of thing going on in South Africa these days."

"Will you stop worrying about him now?"

"Actually, it sounds a little too good to be true, don't you think? I mean how did he find this place, and how did he manage to arrange everything just like—"

"Calm down, Mom, he's been on his own for what, twenty-five years now? Listen, we'll pop down to Durban the day after you get here and we can check it all out. Okay?"

"O-kay. Thanks."

"So, then we'll see you on Thursday, the fifteenth of December?"

I hesitated, wondering if I should say something about Larry's defection.

"Right?" he said.

"Uh, right. Around ten thirty or so, depending on customs."

"We'll be there, jumping up and down and making a scene. Listen, gotta go. Loveyoubye." He waited for me to say the same. We'd adopted his seven-year-old son Daegan's custom of ending our phone conversations.

"Loveyoubye." I hung up and stared up at the ceiling.

My brother. What heartache.

Sweetpea barked and I jumped. She and Jake sat to my right like *His Master's Voice* models, staring at me.

"Greenies!" I jumped to my feet. "I'm so sorry. Come on, let's go get 'em."

Three

I RAN THE bathwater then lay there thinking about my brother, eight years my junior. He was never far from my thoughts. Jiminy Cricket. That's what I started calling him the day he came home from the hospital, a dead ringer for the Disney character: head too big for his bird-like body, all that thick black hair, and when he wasn't crying or vomiting, he chirped. His hair turned into a dark brown as he became older, but his body never quite grew into all that hair. He had thick, lustrous eyelashes and dark liquid eyes that killed when he looked at me in bewilderment. His mental impairment made me anxious all the time. I didn't want him to get his feelings hurt, but mostly I didn't want him to embarrass me.

He didn't have many opportunities to play with other kids, what with an enlarged heart, respiratory problems, and a wide range of severe allergies: grass, milk, mangoes, peanuts, rice, oats, and even sunlight at one point, which made him break out in a rash whenever he was out in the sun. That particular allergy stopped after a while, at least. When he was old enough to eat solids, my mother started feeding him on a plank with his head slightly lower than his body, because if she didn't he'd vomit right away. I can't remember why she had to do this, and my parents aren't around to remind me—all I remember is taking off for the bush when feeding time came, because it made Garth cry and my mother anxious.

And then, when he was eight, Garth had an operation because his ribs were growing into his lungs. I never did understand how something like that could happen. He was cut almost in half, leaving a thick scar that traveled from his right nipple across his chest to the middle of his back. In later years, his misshapen ribs would give him a slightly hunched appearance. At the time we had to travel down to what is now Harare, Zimbabwe—in those days it was Salisbury, Southern Rhodesia—to find surgeons who could perform the operation: seven hundred miles across twisting escarpments and washed-out bridges and down narrow bush roads. For two months we visited Garth whenever my father could get time off from his job as a winding engine driver on Nkana copper mine. We'd drive through the night and spend as much time with Garth as we could, usually curled up on hard wooden chairs beside his bed.

No one expected him to live past twenty. But he'd survived. He'd survived his adored big sister "San"'s emigration to America. He'd even survived our parents' death, which left him on his own save for a nearby uncle and aunt who mostly ignored him. Not only had he survived for twenty-five years, he'd done so fully employed at a government-sponsored job my dad found for him before he died. He also took care of Margaret, a handicapped co-worker whose flat he shared. He'd made it all these years without me. But I hadn't quite made it without him. I carried the guilt of what I'd failed to do for him.

The side door to the garage slammed and I jumped. The bamboo gave a loud sigh. Wind chimes tinkled and clanged wildly: Santa Anas, those hot, crazy-making winds that sometimes blow in from the desert. So that's why I'd been feeling so edgy. Another powerful blast of what some call devil winds whirled around the house, setting off the huge, handcrafted Soleri brass bell we'd hauled from Arizona on the trip we took twelve years earlier—the first time our marriage took an almost fatal dip. Its deep, mournful groan filled the house.

Four

I THOUGHT OF the mess the powerful Santa Anas would leave behind. How fitting. Along with raking up bamboo leaves, bougainvillea blossoms, and wild figs from the vine on the twenty-foot-high wall we shared with the body shop next door, I'd be in intense conversation with my inner psychologist about Larry's latest escape. Those devil Santa Ana winds could whip the smallest ember into a town-leveling fire in no time; they'd done it thirteen years earlier, when the fire barely missed our house. But they could also pump up great waves. Larry had timed his escape just right this time: the waves would be perfect in Mexico. If that's even where he was.

Sweetpea trotted into the room and stretched out on her stomach on the floor next to me, back legs splayed like a frog. Jake followed her, ever-present floppy Frisbee dangling hopefully from his mouth. I started upstairs to get a top and came face to face with a mask of Larry's face, set in a three-foot-high tea-stained jar wedged into a corner of the staircase. I'd hand-built the piece when we first married, inspired by his artistic talent and encouragement to try ceramics myself.

I sank down onto the staircase and touched the nose. Such perfect features for a mask: narrow oval face, straight Indian nose—he was one-quarter Arapahoe, three-quarters Irish/Scot—salt-and-pepper Sam Elliott moustache. Even at thirty-five when I married him, three weeks after we came together in a wild frenzy of sex and feverish togetherness, he was still as good-looking as his Anaheim High School photos revealed. I'd been amazed that this gorgeous, creative man was still available. With his prematurely greying hair, which he kept long, he would turn into a dead ringer for Gandalf, J. R. R. Tolkien's leader of "The Fellowship of the Ring." But he didn't like people calling him that. It took me a long time to realize he hated to be the center of attention. This was someone who seemed to cultivate the limelight.

Late afternoon light shifting through the window glanced off the mask's empty eyes. Eyes so different from those first days when they challenged me to share the joke with him, slate-blue eyes that pulled me in, eyes that I would learn never gave away his thoughts.

"What?" I would smile. He'd shake his head, and then I had to drag it out of him. He'd felt "moony" over me. That's the closest he ever came to silly love talk.

I remember the day I cast his face in plaster of Paris for the mask. He lay on his back on the then-cement front deck, Vaseline smeared all over his face, his beard and moustache matted with the goo. I'd finally persuaded him to go along with my experiment, but he almost lost it when I kept slathering on Vaseline. He couldn't even stand sunscreen on his face. So there he lay, two straws sticking out of his nose, while I kneeled beside him with a bucket of plaster, slapping it on, hoping this was the way it was done. All I knew was that I had to hurry and finish before the stuff set. Just as I was about to plop down the last handful of plaster, he grunted.

I bent over and yelled, "What's wrong?"

Sticking his index finger in his ear as if I'd broken his ear drum, he made a rolling motion with his other hand for me to hurry.

"Yeah, yeah, I'm almost done," I said just as his hand came down on top of mine. Plaster flew everywhere, some of it landing on the end of the straw sticking out of one nostril. He made a snuffling sound and, Frankenstein-like, struggled to get to his feet.

"Wait, wait!" Jumping up, I glanced around desperately for something to clear the straw. A bamboo twig? Too thick. He flopped back down and growled.

I crouched over him. "Snort it out!"

I burst out laughing and couldn't stop. Doubling over, I staggered around, crying with laughter. He reached blindly for me, his growl now a muffled roar.

"Sorry," I managed to gasp, and I kneeled beside him. I touched the plaster. It had set. "Listen, I'm going to get this stuff off right now, it won't be long, okay?" I bit my lip to stop the giggle that bubbled up and started tugging on the edge over his forehead. He roared in pain.

"I told you we needed more Vaseline!" I shouted.

Twenty minutes and a million microscopic tugs later I held a hair-speckled mold of Larry's face in my hands. He sat up and glared at me.

Now I couldn't help the grin that stole across my face. His encouragement had led me to the world of the arts, a world I'd yearned for back in Nkana and didn't know it. The arts back there consisted mostly of tap and ballet classes given either by neophyte ballet teachers or an aging ballerina relegated to the bush. From the age of five I threw myself into both; I did well in ballet, and was being groomed for a spot at Sadler's Wells School of Ballet in England.

But as I grew older I became more and more resentful of all the time I had to spend practicing while my girlfriends were free to roam Nkana on their bikes, looking for boys. I started bunking class and became a juvenile delinquent. This included sneaking out of my bedroom window and hitchhiking along bush roads in the middle of the night with my girlfriends. Sadler's Wells fell by the wayside, and my mother started threatening me with reform school.

Despite my forays into teen wasteland, I still felt the need to do something creative. Only I didn't call it that. All I knew was that there was something inside me that wanted to come out, that had me reaching for a pencil and paper. I couldn't draw worth a damn, but I kept trying, copying Degas's ballerinas, magazine models, Bugs Bunny comics, Pablo Picasso's bull, still life compositions.

When I was fifteen, my dad arranged classes with Mrs. Bingham, the eighty-year-old mother of one of my dad's co-workers on Nkana mine. She'd been one of Queen Elizabeth II's official artists, rendering Her Majesty's intricate proclamations with their tiny gold leaf depictions of fox hunts, deer, and country scenes along the borders. For a year I walked the ten blocks up to Fourth Avenue on Saturday mornings to spend half the day fashioning the alphabet in Old English script and copying pen and ink birds from the English countryside. I loved the precise, ornate structure of the letters, and I loved getting lost in the detail of the fine black lines of the birds' tiny claws, wings, beaks, and eyes, and of the branches on which they perched. I was thrilled by the scratch of the pen against the page. It transported me. And then I got married. And that was that, except for a couple of chalk sketches of my newborn son.

So when this artistic surfer showed up, I was ready. It was his unassuming confidence that impressed me. The way he took up making pots. Just like that. He'd made the decision after learning that a potter friend was selling his equipment to focus on painting instead. He bought most of the guy's gear and before long he was making teapots, coffee mugs, plates, and planters, at one point earning a living from his pottery in Santa Barbara.

He was so different from my first husband, John, the cocky blond and blue-eyed boy who'd swept into little Nkana from Boksburg, South Africa, when I was sixteen.

Me at Sixteen

The eighteen-year-old was a catch, or a "talent," as we used to say. My first love. After three years of hanging around together—including a month-long breakup over John's temper when he accidentally killed my hamster, which had bitten him; his six-month military service in the Federation Army in what is now Zimbabwe; and second thoughts on my part—we finally married. Oh, the wailing from my mother for hitching up with an Afrikaaner, one of those Dutch Calvinist descendants who, with their fundamentalist belief that Africans were lesser beings, were the architects of South Africa's apartheid policy. Still, I think she wanted me out of the house as much I wanted to be out of it. My dad was tight-lipped about the whole thing, but he didn't try to stop me.

Once the novelty of being a wife wore off, I felt trapped. I wanted the single life I never had. I wanted to go to Europe and England with Joan, my girlfriend, like we'd planned when we were fifteen. It didn't help that she went on her own. And why hadn't I stuck with becoming a ballerina, or with my drawing? But by then I was pregnant with my first son, Darin, and things went from bad to worse. We were both way too young. I ignored signs of John's inflexibility and what a friend of mine later called his "short man's complex." At some point I remember telling people I was lucky to have married a man who knew and followed the rules.

Our move to the States three years later—something that had been on my back burner ever since I was ten, and the most ambitious of all my plans—delayed the demise of our marriage by ten years. We landed in Mount Holly, North Carolina, a small town outside of Charlotte; I had enrolled John in a heavy equipment operator program in neighboring Chapel Hill. That first snowfall at the end of the course sent us scurrying for warmer weather—to Southern California, where we knew a couple from Nkana who had emigrated a year earlier. John only briefly used what he'd learned in the course; before becoming a machinest and then a partner in a company that built machines used in automation. I finally decided to end our marriage after he returned from a three week hiatus to "find himself"—while he was gone, I'd realized how much happier I'd been without his bad moods and explosive temper.

My divorce from John wasn't yet final when I met Larry. I had moved out of our Huntington Beach home and had been living on my own for almost a year. I'd hoped we could sell the house so I could support myself, fifteen-year-old Darin, and thirteen-year-old Layne, but John wouldn't hear of it. Because I was the one who had requested the divorce, he truly believed I wasn't entitled to anything. He froze our savings accounts, and the boys stayed with him while our lawyers tried to convince him that I was entitled to half of everything. Finally, after a year, he bought me out. But until then I had to make it on my paltry salary working for John Gildea and Associates, where I drafted schematics for building sites.

Taking my clothes and a favorite frying pan, I moved in with a co-worker in Santa Ana, down the street from work. It was a whole new world for me: I'd never been on my own; I could eat artichokes at midnight if I wanted to. But I felt guilty and selfish for not sticking it out with John for my sons' sakes. Mostly, though, I missed them and worried how they would fare without me. Every morning for a year I made the twelve-mile round-trip to Huntington Beach to get them off to school.

And then I got a job as a Letter Carrier with the United States Postal Service. It meant health benefits and a lot more money. I could no longer get the boys off to school, but we saw each other on the weekends. John and I had joint custody of the boys, and the decision was made for them to stay with him until they finished high school.

A month later, I moved into a subterranean room that had been jury-rigged beneath a three-bedroom house in North Laguna, which in turn was being rented by a young couple who sold marijuana. For $250 a month, I got a hot plate, a tiny shower and toilet, and a ground-level window overlooking a handkerchief-sized slab of cement. My newly purchased queen-size waterbed filled almost the entire room. There was just enough room up front for a white fake animal skin rug and a small table and chair.

I was having an adventure. I felt like a teenager. Plus, I was an employee of the United States Government. The post office was a thrill for me—uniform, eagle insignia, and all.

* * *

Larry started teasing me my second day on the job.

"How many trays of letters have you got to go now?" he called from across the aisle in the twenty-five person carrier bay. There were three bays in the warehouse-sized building. His taunts were met with hoots of laughter as I struggled to find the right address amongst three hundred slots of unfamiliar numbers for each of the thousand letters I had to sort in a certain amount of time without freaking out under the pressure. I had lost seven pounds off an already underweight frame in my first three weeks, I constantly felt at the point of hysteria, and I got lost most days while delivering the mail—but I loved the challenge. It was a whole new world for me: a man's domain where the women who carried mail were expected to be one of the guys. I could do this.

But I hadn't counted on having to deal with this man. His teasing made the job that much harder. Snapping back at him just brought more teasing, along with a collective, exuberant, "Whoa!" from those around us. Mostly I avoided him whenever possible. Yet he had this animal magnetism that drew me in, as well as a preternatural composure, an insouciance topped by a lightning-fast wit that was drop-dead funny. Then there was my sandwich he paid for at the same time he was paying for his at the lunch counter in Ralph's grocery store, where we both happened to be one afternoon on our respective routes. No teasing, no smart aleck remarks, just a generous gesture and we both went on our way. But the teasing continued.

Then, one Tuesday night, a couple of guys from work invited me to Taco Tuesday at Malarkey's, an Irish Pub in Newport Beach. Larry arrived a few minutes after I did, and I found myself sitting next to him at the bar, all six feet of him posing sincere, thoughtful questions about my life. Shy, almost. Vulnerable. And that rich, deep voice. All of it was as confusing as his teasing had been, and completely seductive. I felt betrayed by the thrill that coursed through me. We spent half the night talking on the beach behind Malarkey's, followed by a quick, feverish coupling in the back of his van. We made a dinner date for Saturday night and exchanged phone numbers.

For the next three days we avoided each other at work. I was embarrassed about being so "easy," but I was also thrilled. I couldn't deny my overwhelming attraction to him. I knew it would be a huge mistake to date someone from work—besides, he wasn't divorced yet. What was I thinking? On the other hand, he avoided me because he said he'd felt "weird" about our encounter. I would soon learn that "weird" was a word he often substituted for feelings he couldn't express. But the truly weird thing about it all was that the "gang" at work—mostly the old-timers, guys who could've taken their daily banter, born from the mind-numbing boredom of postal work, to Las Vegas—twigged onto the fact that something was going on with their leader. Suddenly he was quiet. And this one guy, Dave, hopped right on it. He used Larry's favorite line: "Get some last night?"

"Does she use a cane? Have a seeing-eye dog?"

I put off breaking the date until Saturday morning. First I called my cousin—she and her husband had recently emigrated from South Africa—to tell them I was coming to visit for the weekend. Then I called the number Larry had given me—his eldest sister's house, where he was staying with his fourteen-year-old daughter while he looked for a place to live now that he'd left his wife. His daughter answered and seemed to know who I was. I told her to please tell her father that I'd forgotten about a previous engagement and that I wouldn't be able to meet him that night. And then I gave her my cousin's number. Politeness? Hoping he'd call? Probably a little of both.

He drove seventy miles that night to see me, showing up in typical garb: flip-flops, blue jeans, and a long-sleeved flannel shirt, the cuffs and neck revealing tantalizing patches of perfectly curled dark hair, his moustache barely concealing the crooked bottom tooth I wanted to run my tongue over. His salt-and-pepper hair was cut short.

My cousin and her husband, all polite South African graciousness—along with scarcely concealed encouragement—fed us and suggested we head for the Jacuzzi in their apartment complex, along with a couple bottles of Dos Equis beer. Later, wearing panties and one of my cousin's over-sized T-shirts, which came to my knees, I didn't avert my eyes when Larry stripped and slid into the Jacuzzi beside me. We were alone. I'd felt him that fateful night, but I wanted to see all of him. It was too dark, however. I had to settle for the occasional brush against his body as we soaked and talked. After his persistence in the van, he seemed quietly restrained—shy, even, despite all the kissing we did. That would be the last time kissing didn't mean sex for him. He left at two o'clock the following morning; my lips were raw. I fell asleep in a glow of anticipation. I was in love.

I don't remember how the decision was made to get married. Did he ask me? Probably not. We probably joked about it and then just went ahead and did it. At some point I said something like "Let's just go for whatever this is."

What I do remember is waking at midnight with moonlight streaming through the bamboo blinds in my little hippie pad ten days after he moved in with me. The newborn-size teddy bear he'd bought me at this upscale store in South Coast Plaza lolled on the chair by the window, while the expensive antique kimono he'd bought at the same time hung in my curtain-covered closet. The man had taste and style and was very generous. He had molded his body behind mine, right arm wrapped around me, his hand snug beneath my cheek; our legs were intertwined, his big toe and the next forming a "V" over the back of my ankle—"hooked in," he called it. We couldn't get any closer. I'd never felt this kind of intimacy, this kind of connection. He was perfect, so comfortable to be with, so comfortable with himself. Everything was just so absolutely right with the world.

"I love you," I whispered.

"I love you too."

Three weeks later we were married on Avenida Revolución in Tijuana, Mexico above an arcade selling everything from turquoise jewelry to piñatas by an attorney clad in perfectly draped brown pants and white shirt sleeves rolled up just so above his wrists. He told us in a preacher lilt and broken English that we were embarking upon a sacred journey. And then, with arms outstretched like the godfather himself, he told my beloved to kiss his lovely bride. With an embarrassed laugh, Larry gave me a quick kiss and handed the man his $39. We left the two-story building with our official-looking certificate in hand. It was an illegal ceremony; neither of our divorces was final yet. A year later, in June, we made it legal at the Mission in San Juan Capistrano with my best girlfriend as a witness. But we always celebrated the Mexican marriage: March 11th

* * *

Now, remembering our wedding, I was reminded that years had passed since Larry had bothered to celebrate either one of our anniversaries. I

Official Wedding Day

sighed. Still stretched out on the floor next to me, Sweetpea's head came up and she gave me one of her worried looks. I stroked her and she lay back down. My mind strayed back to Larry.

The perfect American man: easygoing, modest, big old accent (born in California, but sounded like a Southerner). From the age of ten I'd dreamed of marrying an American. It started when American Dominican nuns came to Nkana to teach at St. John's Convent Primary School. I was enrolled right away. The best education around, according to my parents—they were American, after all—even if they charged extra because I wasn't Catholic. Those American scenes they had plastered all over our classroom bulletin boards—happy-faced children tobogganing down snow-covered hillsides, cars towing caravans along wide, tarred roads with honest-to-God roadside public toilets—made me ache for that life, where there seemed to be so much variety, so many possibilities. Even though the nuns were strict, there was a certain unconventionality about them, like the time Sister Vincent-Marie rolled up her habit sleeves and played softball in the dirt with us, stopping for a moment to include five African kids who were watching—unheard of. There was also the variety of the nun's art projects, which stimulated something inside me that couldn't be ignored.

And then there were the nuns' accents, rich as melted chocolate compared to our flat, desiccated pronunciations, which I continued to find enthralling despite the way they made me feel about my colonial self—that we were worse than the natives in the villages; they were to be pitied, whereas we were a bunch of ignorant white interlopers. They had a point. Ironically, their derision fed my yearning for a brand-new life in America.

* * *

In the beginning, I loved family events with my American husband's family. They mostly revolved around his antics. He always found ways to stir up things, silly stuff that left everyone weak with laughter. Like the time his twenty-eight-year-old sister bumped, then managed to catch, one of her mother's expensive Lladro figurines before it hit the floor. In typical fashion, Larry called to his mother in the kitchen that *someone* had something to tell her. His sister windmilled her arms in desperation to shut him up. When his mother appeared he repeated his statement, his eyes on the offending sister. She managed to gasp that he was just messing around. His mother—"General," one childhood friend called her—eyed her youngest daughter suspiciously, considered Larry for a moment with that indulgent look reserved only for him, and told her husband to control his son. The poor, sweet, brow-beaten man just smiled. He couldn't control anything, let alone his son. No one wanted to. This kid in a middle-aged man's body was way too much fun.

I enjoyed these fun fests as much as the rest of the family, maybe even more because it felt good to be with the star of the show. But after a while I began to feel that without Larry I had no place in the family. They seemed to like me all right. But they just didn't seem that interested. I don't remember anyone ever asking me one question about my interests, unless it had something to do with Larry, or even my life in Africa like most people did. Their easygoingness and friendliness promised a special kind of intimacy, but they never delivered. After all the years of celebrating their birthdays, they didn't even know how old I was. I put it down to our many differences—in movies, food, music, most things. Plus, I didn't share their history. But it was more than that. Larry later told me that even for him, dealing with his family was like punching into mist: there was nothing solid there, no real contact. "Kind of what it must be like dealing with me," he added with a wry grin.

Five

THIS WHOLE SITUATION with Larry's family made me miss my parents, especially my dad, more than ever. I wondered what they would've made of my new extended family, of Larry. Would they have been able to give me any insight, advice? I think my mother would've been charmed by him, perhaps more so by the fact that I was no longer with John.

I imagined my dad would've appreciated Larry's easygoing way, his humor. Would he have reacted against the barbs? No. I can't imagine Larry letting loose with someone like my dad. What would Larry's family make of my dad? I think they would've got a kick out of him. Charming, funny, and irreverent like Larry—in a different way; he never "picked" on people—my dad could be larger than life sometimes. On our three-month long trip up to East Africa in our tiny Ford Popular (luggage strapped on top) when I was thirteen and Garth was five—with Corky, our African Grey parrot, along for the ride—my dad was befriended by Andre Broussard, a cigar-chomping Belgian whose compound of wild animals was used by American filmmakers to make *Tarzan* and other films set in Africa.

They met in the lounge of a hotel on the shores of Lake Nyasa, in what is now Malawi, where we spent five days in one of the rondavels—circular, thatched rooms—scattered around the main building before we headed for Tanzania. A week later, after inching along one-lane dirt roads that required my dad to stop every so often and clear the mountain of red dust that had built up in front of the car, we hit the one patch of tarmac on the whole trip: a fifty-mile licorice strip of a road that rose and fell toward Mt. Kilimanjaro's snow-capped distant cone. Following the map Andre had penciled on paper ripped from his cigarette packet, we found the turnoff a couple of miles further down the main drag: a battered tin sign with Andre's last name on it. The road wasn't more than a faint impression in the red dirt. The vegetation was sparse all around.

We spent half the day and half the night trying to find the man's spread. At one point, my dad, with the aid of a couple of planks he'd brought along for such an occasion, had to dig the car out of a muddy ravine. And then, inexplicably, there was a fork in the road. No civilization in sight, and no mention of a fork on Andre's map. Swearing and slamming the steering wheel a couple of times, my dad turned left. When the next landmark, an old wagon wheel, didn't appear after ten miles, we turned back and took the right fork. Finally, at around 10:00 p.m., we arrived to a pack of barking dogs whose noise brought out a soused Andre—swinging a kerosene lantern—and one of the servants. Drinks all around in a living room lined with black-and-white glossies of Hollywood stars, including Gordon Scott, who was the current Tarzan; a grinning Cheetah punching a hairy fist into the air; and a number of female stars, all bosoms and teeth.

Around midnight my dad carried me upstairs to a huge bed we would all share. We spent three nights at Andre's and got to see his whole operation: a couple of lions, a serval cat, a number of monkeys, and Sheila, Andre's pet cheetah, who had the run of the place. And then there was this one African who had been mauled by one of the lions. He was missing an arm. The side of his face was a shiny mask of scars, and he had a slitted peephole for an eye. He still tended the animals.

"His bloody fault for getting too close, eh, Jonas," Andre said in his fractured English, lightly cuffing the man behind the head. Jonas grinned and made an agreeable clicking sound with his tongue.

Except for Sheila, all the animals were enclosed in huge wire cages. I've got photos of her sprawled on top of our car, front paw dangling in front of my mother's frozen smile. The cheetah had leapt up as we were getting ready to leave, leaving a dent in the roof. The Belgian took the photo then handed the camera back to my dad.

Two months later, on the same trip, we finally made it up to Kenya, where soon enough my dad got another invitation. This time it was from an old English couple he'd met in the Norfolk Hotel bar in Nairobi. They insisted we spend a week with them on their ranch in the shadow of Mount Kenya. We were almost killed by Mau Maus on our second night there, but that's another story for another time.

I was anxious about my family's first visit to the States, six years after I left Africa. There was the unraveling of my first marriage. I couldn't bear to hear the words "I told you so" from my mother. I was also worried about my parents' "holiday" drinking, my mother's crying jags over my dad's "other women" from twenty years earlier, and their chain smoking. All taking place in a two-bedroom apartment in Westminster, California with an uptight John and four- and six-year-old boys.

I picked up my family at the Los Angeles airport, my heart pounding with love and anticipation and dread. From the moment my dad burst from the plane tunnel in front of my mom and Garth and everyone else, yanking up his sagging pants—he hated anything tight around his waist—his bottom dentures already in his top pocket, he set my nerves on edge. Treating me like I was still fifteen and everyone around him like they were old pals, he stood and gave a loud Scotch toast in the airport lounge to me, his Pearl of Great Price. It was mortifying at the time, but now I would love a redo of that event. This time, I would appreciate his passion and his openness. And his fierce attachment to family. Maybe he could've warned me of what was to come with Larry.

* * *

The phone rang and I jumped. Torn between picking it up and letting the machine take the call, I stood there as the caller started talking.

"Hey, Larry, this is Jonathan, I was just wondering what you were doing."

I eased into the desk chair and listened as the guy rambled on about his day and how he hoped to see Larry on the bus again soon and then he gave his telephone number. "Give me a call, okay, hey Larry?" He rambled on a little longer, gave his telephone number again and hung up.

I sighed. His voice had the same kind of cadence as my brother's. Larry had chatted to the thirty-something guy three years earlier when his van had mechanical problems and he had to ride the bus to and from work for two weeks. Since then, Jonathon had been leaving the occasional message, along with his phone number. Larry's face crumpled every time I told him Jonathan had called. He wouldn't listen to the messages. He didn't know what to say to the guy. It made him feel really really bad, he said. I didn't know what to tell him. I leaned back in the chair. The Pied Piper of Southern California.

My sons, Darin and Layne, fifteen and thirteen when we got married, gained a whole new status with their friends due to their stepfather's cool wit, how he could "rag" on them all equally with such outrageous hilarity. There were nights we'd have at least five boys camped out on the grass in front of our little underground room, nights where nobody got to sleep before midnight. Mr. Cool's favorite trick was to put a dried dog turd or a slug in a couple of the sleeping bags while the boys were out playing.

And then there were the surf trips down to Trestles, his green van rocking from side to side with a group of boys that kept growing. My sons still joke about how they've been permanently scarred by all the crap he put them through. How he'd yank their wetsuits down to their ankles and shove them tottering naked across the beach, usually in front of some bikini-clad beauty. And the time he rocked the portable outhouse at the beach with Layne in it, almost tipping it over.

Here was a father who was one of them, who on so many levels was a buddy, someone who never lost his temper or handed out angry ultimatums like their father had. But it was Darin who grew more and more resentful about Larry's teasing. That's because Larry could get a bigger rise out of him than his brother. Layne learned to roll with it.

A twenty-something woman at work, someone who had a crush on Larry, once confessed to me that it was weird how he could sometimes hit a nerve with his teasing, like he had a sixth sense about some current or existing vulnerability of hers—but she refused to believe that he meant to hurt her. Another girlfriend told me how she'd felt "brutalized" more than once by how he would hone in on her dating life, knowing it wasn't going well. His sisters and daughters had stories of how he teased them until they became hysterical. And then there was the time he wouldn't let up on his brother-in-law, who, goaded to the point of desperation, floored his van down the block with Larry clinging to the side. He, too, didn't hold it against Larry.

Because this was the guy everyone thought of as their particular pal, who had what one friend called an essential sweetness. I mean, this was a man who couldn't pass a homeless person without a generous donation and a kind word. Who would chat for hours with the guy everyone else avoided because he was an asshole or a bore. And those Seventh Day Adventist missionaries, how they loved him. One of them ended up dropping by every couple of weeks just to talk about cars. Outside the gate, of course—Larry never invited anyone in.

It was a head-spinner for me. I constantly found myself in a dilemma over this "other" side of him, the goading, aggressive side. It was like he'd taken leave of his senses. When I got mad or hurt by his aggressiveness, he'd make a face like I'd lost my mind, telling me I was way too sensitive. I half-believed him. Especially since he only teased people he liked, or so he said. Mostly I believed he felt emotionally vulnerable and teasing gave him some kind of control, a way to keep people at bay, while at the same time it allowed him to feel something. It was like he fed on the emotional distress of others. I could never decide if he truly believed that he was "just playing" like he insisted he was.

What puzzled me was how someone kind and generous in so many ways couldn't see the effect his teasing had on others. But I expected that with my love and help he'd come to realize that what he was doing was cruel and harmful. I continued to believe this even after the time he goaded me to the point where I flipped out and almost killed him with an X-Acto knife.

It happened seven years into our marriage. I'd told Larry about a conversation I'd had with this guy at work about spirituality. I thought he would appreciate the sentiments expressed.

Instead, he launched in with, "You're in love with him, aren't you?"

"What?" I hardly knew the guy.

"Why don't you just admit it?"

"Are you serious?"

"Come on, be honest now."

"Stop messing around."

"You love him, don't you?"

"Okay, what's going on?"

"You tell me." There was something in the way he said this, a lilt to his voice. Was he "just playing?" I thought about how he'd once told me I was easy to tease because I took things so seriously.

"I don't understand," I said.

He stared at me, like he was waiting for me to confess. Despite myself, I couldn't help wondering if he was picking up on something I myself didn't even know. The thought unnerved me. We went back and forth, the conversation growing more and more insane, with him jabbing at me with insinuating questions. The angrier I became the calmer he grew. It was like he was watching a movie, curious to see what came next.

Finally, feeling overwhelmed and frantic, I flung the knife into the doorway just inches above his head and then stood there, glaring at him, with my hands clenched. His mouth dropped open in that way he had of showing exaggerated surprise. He did a slow pan from me to the knife then back again.

"You tried to kill me," he whispered.

I stared at him, my anger trickling away, replaced by guilt and frustration and fear.

"Didn't you?" he insisted.

"Enough, okay?" I cried.

"Well, you did."

Feeling the rush of tears, I pushed past him. He made an exaggerated staggering motion backward. "Remind me not to mess with you again."

Six

THE ONLY TIME Larry referred, albeit obliquely, to my knife-throwing episode was after an incident that happened the following week. I was still shaken about what had happened. We were on our way back from buying clay at a pottery supply place in Santa Ana and, without knowing exactly where we were, we'd stopped in Buena Clinton—the gang capital of Orange County at the time—to get beer.

With Larry carrying two bottles of beer, we headed for the counter to pay. Ahead of us, two twenty-something guys with slicked-back hair and identical black sleeveless T-shirts and pants with a long silver chain hanging from one pocket were hassling the middle-aged Vietnamese man behind the cash register. A six-pack of Budweiser sat on the counter.

"Speak fuckin' English, *pendejo*," the shorter of the two men said.

His face expressionless, the clerk said something in fractured English.

Shorty leaned on the counter, cocked his head toward his companion with a how-much-more-of-this-shit-can-I-take expression, then turned back to the clerk.

"Okay, now, let's take this slowly eh, *estúpido*?"

"Don't be such a bully," I said, stepping up to the counter. "Can't you see he's doing the best he can?"

I felt Larry take a couple of steps backward. Shorty and his companion did a slow motion turn, glanced at Larry, looked at each other, then turned back to me.

"This *our* turf," Shorty said.

"How much is the Budweiser?" I asked the clerk. While not sorry I had stepped forward, I felt a prickle of fear.

I couldn't be sure, but I thought the clerk said $5.65. Without looking at the two guys, I repeated this amount. The clerk didn't correct me. Reaching into his pocket, Shorty pulled out a money clip and peeled off three dollars then turned and glared at his friend.

"Hey, *vato*, what you waiting for?"

The guy threw down three dollars. The clerk made change.

Gathering the coins, Shorty cocked his head in my direction, his mouth twisted in a hard smile. "We see you again, lady, you not so lucky."

Nodding his agreement, his companion gave me a searing look, grabbed the six-pack, and together they swaggered toward the door.

Larry slid the two bottles of beer onto the counter. "You could've gotten me killed."

"Thanks for having my back."

"That was dumb," he said, paying for the beer. We headed for the door.

"Weren't you worried about me?" I said.

He grinned, hooked an arm around my neck, and kissed me on the side of the head. "It was them I was worried about. They would've kicked my ass. But *no* one dare mess with you, right, Para?"

His greeting cards were genius. I once told him I wished I could take a peek into his brain to see how everything was arranged in there. His cards were funny, original, and right on the mark when they referred to some obscure, forgotten detail that would make the sourest face break into a grin. The cards to me always had some reference to sex.

For our ninth anniversary he purchased a card with the words "THANKS COACH" printed in garish, blue-outlined red words across a bright yellow background. Inside he'd handwritten: "My loved One, thank you for the best nine years of my life. I guess I still just like you, even though I would like to get in your pants a little more and score on the beasties. But I've survived, my teacher of the Untainted Wisdom of Life and Beholder of the Dickless Hump. You are a marvel. You make me look too good. It is so easy to be with you. I love you, my Para." There was an oily smear below this and the words: "Guess what was dabbed in mineral oil and impressed as a lasting signature? Pity Z." I knew the smear came from his penis dabbed in oil.

Para, long "a": his pet name for me, after Paraquat Kelley, a disk jockey on KMET whose rock n' roll selections blared through the post office in the 80s. At the time, the American government was spraying marijuana crops in Mexico with paraquat, a lethal herbicide. Mr. Kelley added the tag as a protest against this practice. I'm not sure why Larry started calling me Paraquat in the beginning, but the moment he saw it annoyed me, he kept going.

The name evolved into Bo Para (after Bo Derek—you're *my* number ten) and then just Para, which stuck. Signing himself Pity Z was a distortion of my calling him Pretty Thing, plus his affinity for Zen Buddhism. Later birthday cards he signed "Pitiful Z" or "The Asshole."

In the beginning I loved his habit of making off-the-wall comments to anyone from the grocery store checker to co-workers and friends. People who knew him looked to me to see if whatever remark he'd just made was true: So he's not part Hawaiian, then? So he never went to 'Nam? So you don't have a wooden leg? You never worked in a circus? I'd grin, roll my eyes, and shake my head. Years later, after he transferred to another post office twenty miles away, one of his co-workers came up to me and, with an incredulous expression on her face, doubled over laughing. "You're *not* a midget." Funny stuff.

But on too many occasions his comments just weren't funny. Sometimes they seemed like some obscure joke only he knew about. Like the time we went to South Africa. The humor there is similar to that of the Brits, but a little more down-to-earth and without nuance. They can be a serious bunch, especially the older generation, like my aunt and uncle whom I hadn't seen since John and I honeymooned down their way.

"They're not going to get your humor, I'm telling you," I warned Larry. "You're just going to confuse them and embarrass me if you pull any of your shit."

Half an hour into our reunion in a quaint little bed and breakfast outside of Umhlanga Rocks on the east coast of South Africa, we're having a beer, my aunt and uncle a cup of tea. When it comes time to pay, Larry announces to the African waiter, "I'm not allowed to have my own money."

The waiter freezes, gives a nervous smile; my aunt and uncle exchange puzzled glances. I force a laugh, tell them he's only playing, fumble in my wallet, hand the waiter a wad of cash, and glare at Larry. My uncle and aunt stare down at their hands, clear their throats, glance outside. Moments later they recover, thank us, and continue talking about old times like the incident never happened.

I blasted Larry later.

"Why do you care what people think?" he said.

I did care what people thought, maybe more than most—especially in South Africa.

Seven

THE BABOON WAS called Archie; the Vervet monkey, Jo-Jo; the bush-baby—a tiny, pop-eyed nocturnal creature—Little One. The latter lived in my bedroom when I was a teenager, Jo-Jo outside in a big cage. They were animals I'd begged my father to rescue from Congolese traders peddling monkeys and parrots alongside the roads of the Copperbelt. That's where we got Corky, the parrot, who my mother trained to bite my toes because I wouldn't wear shoes. All these poor creatures were almost always starving, some of them barely a couple of weeks old, after being taken from mothers who'd been killed for their babies. But Archie was already a couple of years old when we got her from a neighbor.

Other than all the animals I was always rescuing, it was Leffy, our Bemba manservant—six feet tall and blacker than black—with whom I spent most of my time during my formative years. He was probably in his late twenties. Everyone had servants, men who came in from the villages in search of work in the houses or gardens. My mother emerges in my memory around this time as a distant, solitary figure who, when she wasn't crocheting, knitting, or sewing clothes for herself and me, devoured books, whatever our little library in the Mine Club had in stock. My dad was either working—sometimes sixteen hours a day or night—or trying to get some sleep. Or spoiling me.

At the time we lived on Tenth Avenue in "old" Nkana, before the little mining town spread down to the Kafue River power station. This was before Northern Rhodesia became Zambia, before Southern Rhodesia became Zimbabwe. We'd moved there from South Africa when I was eighteen months old so my father could take advantage of the copper boom in the mines that had sprouted in the bush ten years earlier. Like the three hundred other white families who worked for Rhokana Corporation Mining Company, we lived in a furnished brick house with a corrugated tin roof, wood-burning stove, and generous-sized yard filled with jacaranda, frangipani, mango, guava, loquat, and avocado trees. And bougainvillea—there was always bougainvillea.

At three I knew more Bemba than I did English. Leffy also taught me how to shoot a spit ball and how to whistle through my tongue, making the haunting sounds of an owl. He also taught me to play Stones, a game like American Jacks, in holes carved out of the hardscrabble dirt in front of his *kiya*, a brick room at the bottom of our backyard. Inside, his iron bed perched atop a stack of bricks to keep him safe from the *tokoloshi*, those hairy creatures of the underworld that would gouge out the eyes and bite off the toes of those sleepers they could reach. Squatting beside his fire, I ate *sadza* with him, scooping up enough of the thickened cornmeal porridge with my fingers to mold a fat thumb shape, then, making a dent in the middle, I would dip the *sadza* into his enamel bowl of pork grease before shoving the whole thing into my mouth, grease dripping down my chin.

One time I helped him gather these big, plump worms from the trees (and off the ground if they weren't too squashed—it was during the rainy season), and then sat with him while he fried them over the fire in his big black pot. It took me about five attempts to get one of those crispy little twists into my mouth, while he held his stomach and rolled around on the ground with laughter at the expression on my face. They did taste like bacon, but all I could think about was how they'd wriggled around, all squishy in my fingers, when I helped gather them. It was my first and last worm-eating experience.

Leffy had this odor, a combination of his musk, native tobacco, and wood smoke that I found stinky at the time but now remember with fondness. When I started kindergarten, he was the one who took me to Frederick Knapp School on the back of his bike on a special seat he'd made for me out of scraps of leather, cloth, and wire.

Later, when we returned to Nkana from South Africa, where my brother was born, Leffy found us and started working for us again. Once, when I was eleven, my mother locked me in the bathroom. I'd probably mouthed off to her, or maybe I'd made and ate an entire bowl of raw cookie dough while she napped—a favorite infraction of mine. Leffy helped me climb out of the window, bending over so I could lower myself down onto his back.

She discovered me an hour later in the back lane playing Stones with him. Grabbing me by the arm, she whacked me on the bottom and was about do so again when Leffy rose to his feet and in an apologetic voice told my mother it wasn't good for *picannin missus* to be locked up. Whether shocked at his audacity or touched by it, she gave me another half-hearted whack and then shoved me toward the house.

"Your *picannin missus* is a very naughty girl," she said over her shoulder as she followed me.

Looking back, I wonder what he thought of this spoiled little girl who sometimes ordered him around, who rarely thanked him, who had him keep a lookout while she did something she wasn't supposed to. I can still remember how nervous this made him, because he would also get into trouble if I got caught. Did he resent the way I just wandered in and out of his *kiya* anytime I wanted to, how I got mad at him for not knowing where I'd left something of mine—my school hat or tie, a favorite blouse, my ruler? Did I ever share my cookie dough with him?

My parents were good employers: they didn't make him stay late into the night whenever they threw a party, like most others did; they let him off whenever he needed to visit his family in his village. They also allowed his two wives to visit him in his *kiya*—one at a time. Leffy caught hell from one or the other if they happened to show up at the same time. Looking back, what I remember is his devotion to me. Always ready to lie for me to protect me from my mother—like the time I sneaked out of the house to play with Archie, the female baboon who I'd named after my dad.

It was a December afternoon at the peak of the hot season. I was five. The air was thick with flies and the thrum of crickets. Arms draped over my knees, I sat slumped in the dirt at the bottom of the yard, Archie on her haunches behind me, probing my head for fleas. We sat half-hidden behind the old doghouse, which she was tethered to by a ten-foot chain attached to a belt around her waist. I wasn't allowed to be alone with Archie. Baboons could be possessive and unpredictable. Even a suspicion of a bite and it was curtains for Archie and rabies shots for me—two a day for seven days. In the stomach. But I wasn't afraid. I knew she wouldn't bite me. She was my best friend. Leffy sat snoozing in his rickety, straight-backed chair, propped against the wall of his *kiya*, way across the yard, unaware of what I was up to. I can still feel Archie's long, black-tipped fingers scratching through my hair, the goose bumps marching up and down my arms and back as she searched for fleas. Those soothing clicking sounds she made, the frantic scratching when she thought she'd found one.

"*Missi!*" I jerked up to see Leffy glaring at me, hand outstretched.

Archie shrieked and grabbed me from behind, half hopping onto my back. Arms flailing, I tried to swing around, but she was too heavy. Leffy grabbed the rake propped against the mango tree and raised it above his head. I twisted onto my side. Archie rolled off my back into the dirt. Leffy brought down the rake, just missing her as she scrambled into the doghouse. A car door slammed in the driveway. My dad, home from work. I scrambled to my feet, ran across the yard, and, bursting into tears, charged into his arms.

"What's this, now?" my dad asked, gently untangling himself.

I blubbered something about falling and getting hurt. He made comforting sounds and carried me toward the house. My mother stood waiting for us in the doorway, and after seeing I was okay, she glanced toward Archie's doghouse, a suspicious gleam in her eyes. Head down, Leffy stood under the mango tree, raking.

"Leffy, was the *picannin missus* playing with Archie?" she called.

"*Aikona Medem!*" he said indignantly and continued to rake.

I got a chiding from Leffy later. Archie got to live, though I don't know for how long, because we gave her to the family next door six months later when we left for Southern Rhodesia.

We lived in Southern Rhodesia for eighteen months while my dad managed Mr. Bradley's sisal plantation. The twenty-acre plantation was seventy miles from the closest town; and the only people I remember were Mr. and Mrs. Bradley and their three boys.

After that, we moved to Rustenburg for a while, then Welkom, a dusty gold mining area in the eastern part of South Africa where Garth was born. Then it was on to Alpine Valley, near Barberton, site of the late-1880s gold rush where some of the earth's oldest and best preserved rocks and first life forms had been discovered. My dad worked on the mines and made bricks part-time for a man who lived down the hill in a big house with a swimming pool, someone he called Mister. He would sometimes walk me through the bush to have tea with Mary, the man's daughter. Two hours later, he'd return and we'd walk home hand in hand. But other than that I didn't have any friends. Mostly I helped my dad and his workers make bricks or hiked the hills with him looking for old abandoned mine shafts when he had time off, which wasn't often. My mother was consumed with taking care of a sickly Garth.

One day I went for a Sunday drive with a family who lived down the street from us. My mother insisted. I was still new to the small community nestled in the hills. There was the mom and dad, a girl my age, and her younger brother. They were Afrikaans, religious and dour—maybe they saw in me a lost sheep they hoped to bring into the fold. My dad said they were sourpusses. The children wore shoes and socks; I was barefoot as usual, at the last moment slipping off the shoes and hand-knitted socks my mother had insisted I wear. I wore one of my mother's hand-made dresses. At some point in the hour-long journey, we stopped to take in the view. As soon as I spotted an ice cream

Me and Garth in Alpine Valley

man and his cart on the side of the road, I was out of the car, running to buy an ice cream sandwich. My dad had given me sixpence for just such an occasion.

Surely I must've asked permission, along with the requisite "please" and "may I?" I must've remembered that much from my mother's constant hammering. Perhaps not. Or had I taken their shocked silence for consent? Ice cream from ice cream carts was always permitted by my father, but not so for the Calvinistic Dutch Reformed Church members, where such indulgences were frowned upon. Why didn't I realize that something wasn't right when the kids didn't follow me?

I bought my ice cream, got my tickey change, and strolled back toward the car focused on taking that first crisp bite through the two wafers and frozen vanilla ice cream. Rolling the confection around in my mouth to minimize an ice cream toothache, I slid onto the car seat and shut the door behind me. I took another bite and stopped.

The kids, perched on the edge of the backseat like two predatory birds, stared at me in stunned silence. I risked a glance at the two grown-ups in the front seat. More stares, hard and disapproving. Dropping my gaze to the floor, I slumped. I shouldn't have charged off like that. I shouldn't have bought the ice cream. Was I supposed to buy everyone an ice cream? The car started and we were back on the road. Face on fire, I kept my head down, trying to minimize the movement of my jaw as I rolled and chewed and swallowed. My first impulse was to stuff the ice cream into my dress pocket, get the offending thing out of sight. But it would melt and drip on the seat. The kids continued to stare at me.

"Want some?" I whispered, holding out the ice cream.

Shooting anxious glances toward their parents they shook their heads, more of a shimmy really, like they didn't want to be caught acknowledging my offer.

I hunched over to make myself as small as possible, jammed the rest of the ice cream sandwich into my mouth and chewed as fast as I could before gulping down large pieces. Stabbing pain between my eyes. I stifled a cough and prayed I wouldn't throw up. A lifetime later, we drew up in front of my house.

I leapt from the car. "Danke, Meneer, danke Mevrou." I never saw the family again.

eight

ON THE APPOINTED day, I took Sweetpea for her scan while Larry went surfing. Turned out it *was* ectopic ureter. And there was also a problem with her right kidney.

"This is way too complicated for us," Dr. G said. "I went ahead and arranged a consultation with that surgeon I told you about. She's excellent."

Larry accompanied Sweetpea and me to the appointment the following week. There he was, hands clenching and unclenching, saying yeah before I finished my sentences, like he did when functioning on one cylinder. I focused on Sweetpea, who, ecstatic at an entire room of prospects, human and dog, was straining this way and that on her leash, almost yanking me off my feet in her attempts to make contact. With each ecstatic burst forward or sideways, there was a little spurt of pee. I thought Larry was going to bolt. I got a wad of paper towels from the receptionist, despite her reassurances that someone would get it with a mop.

The compact, no-nonsense woman surgeon, forefinger pressed to her lips, gazed down at Sweetpea. "A *very* interesting case." Larry and I exchanged glances. Sweetpea, oblivious to our distress, strained to lick her hand and produced a spurt of pee. I quickly wiped it away with the paper towels.

"After I get done reconnecting those ureters, her leakage should be reduced by at least seventy-five percent," she added, stepping out of reach of Sweetpea's tongue.

I could barely contain my excitement—no mention of the right kidney. "Great!"

"My biggest concern is that other kidney."

I reached for Larry's hand. He squeezed mine. I glanced at him. His face revealed nothing. She didn't elaborate, and we were too afraid to ask. Surgery was scheduled for the following week. We returned home, not saying much.

As if sensing a little comedic relief was needed, Sweetpea went into her wild puppy routine the moment we entered the house. Ears back, she tore around the kitchen and then dove into her bed. Head tucked between her paws, butt in the air, she gazed up at us.

My eyes filled with tears. I turned to Larry, hoping he would tell me she was going to be fine like he had before. But his face was impassive. He stared down at her for a moment, then turned and headed for his pottery studio. I knew I wouldn't see him for the next couple of hours. I sighed and tried not to be resentful.

The night before Sweetpea's operation, Larry slept with his back to me. I lay beside him, tense and sleepless, wanting him to hold me but afraid to reach out, afraid he'd pull away. I finally fell asleep just before the alarm went off.

The morning of Sweetpea's operation, the overcast sky matched my mood. Sweetpea tore into the waiting room ahead of us, her muscled body wriggling furiously. She went with the attendant without a backward glance. Everything is going to work out, I told myself.

"Well, at least *she's* not worried," Larry observed dryly.

An hour and a half later, the surgeon returned to the waiting room. We leapt to our feet. I searched her face as she walked toward us wearing a pensive expression.

"Surgery went very well." She smiled.

"Yes!" I said.

"Only thing, that left kidney, it was too far gone. I had to take it out before it infected the good one."

I felt myself sagging. Larry stared at her.

"Hey, it's not that bad, lots of dogs live a long time with one kidney. But I must warn you, she's not out of the woods yet."

"So when can we take her home?" Larry asked.

"In about four days. We need to monitor her kidney and urine levels. Oh, and one more thing. You're going to have to give her fluids intravenously for the rest of her life, probably three or four times a week. A sort of animal dialysis."

I glanced at Larry. No way would he go for this.

"No problem," he said without hesitation.

"Good," the surgeon said with a curt nod.

The day finally arrived for us to pick up Sweetpea. Instead of the mad dash she'd made into the place, she emerged from the back offices straining against a bright pink leash held by a grinning male assistant. But then four feet away, as if finding hidden reserves, she did her Blues Brother's routine in a mad scramble toward us. Larry dropped to his knees and she hit him in the chest.

"Whoa!" the assistant cried, releasing the leash. "Those stitches!"

"Hey baby girl," Larry murmured, lifting her up into his arms. Wriggling around, paws tucked under against his chest, she planted her chin over his shoulder and grinned at me.

* * *

I thought Larry would abandon both me and Sweetpea the first time we had to stick the needle into the fleshy part of her neck. But he didn't. While I paced and cried and flapped my hands, he told me it would be okay. He made the first attempt.

Those first six months were agonizing; each time, we failed to get more than a couple of drops of solution into her before she dashed out of our grasp. At times I wanted to drive her to the vet and let them do it. Larry never wavered. We gradually grew adept at administering the solution. It was our agitation and fear of failing that set her off. But then, she, too, became more and more comfortable with the process over time, sometimes falling asleep while the solution dripped into her.

No matter what else was going on in our lives, these treatments brought all three of us together. Shortly after Sweetpea turned one, Larry said something that made me realize just how deeply she had affected him. It was during one of her treatments. He sat next to her on the floor, slouched against the wall, stroking and gazing at her with a "moony" expression on his face. I sat a short distance away with my computer on my lap, working on a story about Sweetpea.

"You ruined my life when you got Sweetpea," he said without looking up. "You know that, don't you?"

He looked so vulnerable staring down at her, I felt my heart go out to him. "It's hell caring, isn't it?"

He gave me a sad smile. "I don't like it."

Not long after this, he started to call her "The dog that saved our marriage."

But in the end, he'd left both of us. And now I had to perform Sweetpea's treatment alone. He knew how much I hated that. Who would take care of her and Jake if I wanted to take a trip somewhere? What if I died in a car accident? I hung the bag of fluids and hooked up Sweetpea. I waited until she settled down, then reached into our antique trunk and removed a couple of journals from the stack I'd amassed over the past twenty-eight years, journals filled with insights I'd gained in meditation as well as my frustrations with Larry. I'd been flipping through them ever since the first time Larry left, eight months earlier. Outside, the bamboo whooshed and groaned. The Santa Ana winds were here for a while. A pot crashed to the ground. Was that one of his? Could it be glued back together?

Nine

TWO WEEKS AFTER Larry's disappearance, I lay on the couch sand-wiched between Sweetpea and Jake. It was around two in the morning. I didn't hear the key slip into the front door lock. But the dogs did. Bark-ing, they shot up, untangled, and tore off the couch. The light blazed on in the kitchen. Barking turned into happy Staffie yodeling accompanied by the staccato of their nails against the hardwood floors. A man's deep voice murmured endearments. After a moment of confusion and fear, I realized Larry was home.

Heart pounding, I lay paralyzed by conflicted feelings—rage, along with a tiny nub of hope that he would rush into the room and drop to his knees beside me. I heard the entourage head for the bathroom—the gurgle of the toilet, the rush of water in the washbasin—and then back into the kitchen. The fridge door opened and closed. Any minute now, he would come into the living room to claim the couch, his "bed." I sat up and then lay back down again. I heard the back door close with a soft but solid snap. Thick silence filled the house. Sweetpea and Jake clicked back into the room and stared at me. I stared back. What the hell?

I spent the rest of the night with a piano roll of old standards playing over and over in my mind—words I should've said, words I shouldn't have said, guilt over all my nagging for him to talk to me, our dead-end conversations. And then, way down a cold and windy passage in my mind that I'd worked hard to seal off, her name echoed. Had he started seeing her again? Is that where he'd been for the last ten days? All those other times? And then I was remembering the time I finally said "No" to him.

* * *

It was over sex. One of those incidents that became a dividing point for every other occasion in our marriage. I really meant it this time.

"You're lucky I still want that little body of yours," he said. This was just before his affair. That didn't hurt my feelings. Not one bit. I was too irritated. An affectionate touch from me, or merely being naked—these meant sex, whether I wanted it or not. It had always been that way, only now I wasn't making excuses for him or finding ways to accommodate him. I'd had it.

"You know you want it," he'd say, grinning at his awful cliché. He was a good lover, once he got his way, but I felt like a performing monkey. Sometimes I'd have spontaneous orgasms in my sleep.

The first time I spurned his advances, I didn't really say "No" to sex. It was more like a long-winded, apologetic begging off. This was a week after we moved in together. The next morning he left for work earlier than me, which was not unusual—we had different hours at the time—but when I got to work I learned he'd called in sick. I wanted to charge all over the countryside looking for him, but I didn't even know where to begin. Hell, I didn't know what to think. He returned home that afternoon, cool and calm. It turned out he'd gone surfing and fallen asleep on the sand. He seemed genuinely touched I'd wanted to go looking for him. He called the incident his running-away episode. "See what happens when you refuse me?" he joked. I didn't realize just how much he relied on sex to "get close."

Believing that sex was the only way he could express affection, I kept giving in to Larry's persistent advances. I kept overriding my feelings because I didn't trust myself, because I didn't know where to draw the line. It didn't help when on those occasions I did beg off he'd ask why I didn't like sex, if maybe I was just "cold." Then I'd think about my mother, and I would wonder if he was right.

So on this particular night, he'd followed me up to bed after I told him sex was out of the question because I was still hurting from a vaginal infection. He'd been stalking me like he did sometimes—grabbing my breasts, pinning me to the wall, the kitchen cabinets, sneaking up on me while I got undressed. I pleaded with him to stop, and started to cry. He backed off.

Later, he came up to the bedroom, where I was reading, and started in again. Something inside me snapped, blurring the edges of my vision. I went nuts. Pounding the bed with my fists, I yelled "No, no, no!" over and over again. He drew back and stared at me, his eyes flat; then, without a word, he rose and headed downstairs, where he spent the night on the couch. Things cooled between us after that. From what I can figure, it was shortly after this episode that he had the affair. He claimed that he wanted to tell me about it after it happened, but I was being a bitch and he decided to hell with it.

What had that shrink told me after I found out about the affair? "He shot you—metaphorically speaking—and he's not going to confess. Maybe he never will. He just doesn't have it in him. It's up to you to remove the bullet and heal yourself."

Ten

AT 5:00 A.M., exhausted and bleary-eyed, I dragged myself to work. Twenty years earlier I had transferred from carrying mail to administration. I'd toyed with the idea of calling in sick. On top of everything else, work had become worse than drudgery. The atmosphere was depressing. The Postal Service was downsizing; people were being made "redundant." At least I could retire if I wanted to, but I was eighteen months short of full retirement, and it would mean less money. I was going to hang on. On the way to my office I stopped at my long-time co-worker Chris's office. I stepped in and slumped against the doorjamb.

He glanced up from his computer and grimaced sympathetically. "You're looking good."

I sighed. "I can't take it anymore."

"Surfer dude?"

"He came home last night and then turned around and left again. At two-frigging-o'clock in the morning, for God's sake. Not one word. Nothing."

"Maybe he's finally gone off the deep end."

I sighed. "I don't know. I mean that first trip, well, just between you and me I could've almost gone along with it. Almost. At least he wasn't watching daytime TV. Showed there was some life in him."

"Hey, what's wrong with daytime TV?"

"Lone Ranger? Matt Dillon? He's always hated old shows. Besides, what about all that pottery he was going to make once he retired? The unfinished studio? His Big Plan?"

"Maybe he's reverting to his childhood."

"He does say that those were simpler times. But what's really depressing is that he watches those shows in the dark."

"For you, perhaps."

"Hey, whose side are you on?"

He laughed. "Didn't you tell me that he wasn't being such a dick lately?"

"Well, yeah, he hasn't been badgering me as much. He's even been more engaged. Well, sort of. He's been doing more around the house, the grocery shopping, Sweetpea's appointments . . ." I trailed off, remembering that his lack of affection hadn't changed. But then, I had been nagging him about lying around. And I'd never really let him forget about the affair, and I'd never forgotten how I slapped him soon after I found out, when he kept stonewalling me.

"And why shouldn't he? Hell, he's retired."

"Sometimes I just feel so sorry for him," I said. "He seems so . . . lost."

Chris rolled his eyes. "What about you? Funny how quickly you can forget that mean streak of his."

"Thanks, Chris. Reality check."

"You know, whatever he's going through, I've got to tell you, this whole Mexico thing is pretty damn cold."

I nodded numbly, made some excuse about getting coffee, and headed for my office.

Two hours later, my eldest stepdaughter called. "Has he shown up yet?" she asked in a hard, tight voice. Married, with a son and daughter, she lived fifteen miles away in a neighboring town. She'd been through a lot with her mother's abandonment when she was thirteen and her father's half-assed parenting efforts afterward. After kidnapping her two younger sisters, her mother had split for parts unknown with the carpenter she and Larry had hired to make changes to their house in Big Bear, a resort in the mountains where the family lived at the time. This was months before I took up with Larry. It took the eldest of the two kidnapped girls seventeen years of detective work to find Larry and the rest of the family as she and her sister were dragged around California and the northwest. That's when Larry and I drove up to northern California in the "Love Cage" for the reunion.

Without apology or admitting to any wrongdoing, Larry's ex-wife eased back into her eldest daughter's life with a hippie dippy attitude of the past is the past, just let it go, what matters is that we're family. But the scars were deep, and as far as I knew my eldest stepdaughter had never forgiven her mother and desperately craved her father's attention.

I filled her in on what had happened, trying to keep the bitterness out of my voice.

"What about me?" she asked in the monotone I was used to.

The question threw me. And then it struck me: Larry's escapes weren't just affecting me. It was another abandonment for her.

"I'm so sorry," I said. "I didn't even think about what this must be doing to you. But listen, try not to take it personally. It pisses me off no end, but I think he's just trying to find his way, you know, what with retirement, his mom's death—"

"Bullshit," she said flatly.

We talked for a few more minutes, she said she'd come by, and I hung up, knowing she probably wouldn't. The accustomed feeling of futility I experienced after talking to my stepdaughter settled over me. She was hard to get close to, so like her father. Sometimes it felt like we'd just been introduced for the first time. I regretted not being more of a force in her life, like I wanted to when Larry and I first married. Instead, I had selfishly followed his lead; it was so much easier that way, what with having to deal with my sons' delinquent behavior after their father renounced them, along with Larry's irresponsible behavior when it came to any of the kids. I'd so wanted us all to be a family. Wasn't life supposed to get easier now?

I stumbled through the rest of the day, daydreaming about a nice long hike in the hills with the dogs when I got home.

* * *

The headache that had dogged me all day had receded a little, but the nausea was back. I kicked the car door shut behind me and headed for the house. I knew before I reached for the gate that the wayward traveler was back. I could feel it.

I found him hunched over the pond, kneeling on one of the rocks that encircled it, filter pump in hand. His long grey hair, usually drawn back in a ponytail, hung loose over his shoulders, creating a ghostly effect with the afternoon sun behind him. He glanced up as I entered, slate-blue eyes devoid of expression, body relaxed. He appeared as though this was just any other day, as if he'd just returned from a trip to the store for milk. Still holding on to the gate handle, I stared at him, the thud of my heart loud in my ears. The moment stretched between us. He was waiting for me to say something.

I closed the gate, setting off the attached Tibetan prayer bells. Sweetpea and Jake flew from the house and barreled into me, knocking my bag off my shoulder. Avocados rolled across the deck, followed by my teacup and vitamin pill box from my bag. I let the rest of my stuff fall onto the deck and dropped down to hug and scratch the two dogs. My hands shook.

"They're always so happy to see you," he said mildly, straightening. "They're not like that with me."

As usual, I found myself wanting to respond to his self-deprecation with soothing words. *They love you just as much as they love me. They're just excited because my arrival is a new event in their day.* I caught myself and rose to my feet, head throbbing.

"Just what the hell are you doing?"

He held up the filter. "This thing's filthy."

I glared at him.

"You didn't clean it," he continued.

"I don't know *how* to clean the filter. I shouldn't have to clean the filter. I've never had to clean the filter before," I said, my voice rising. "Besides, it was your bright idea to do the whole pond thing." I stopped myself. "But that's not the point—"

"Yes, you do," he said. "I showed you how."

"Forget the fucking filter. Talk to me. Please. Please just tell me what's going on with you. I mean the way you just take off and then no phone call, no nothing. Anything could've happened to you. Seriously. I had absolutely no way of knowing whether you were dead or alive."

"That's not such a bad thing, is it?" He unscrewed one end of the filter and peering into it, scraped out pond scum with his fingers.

"What, you being dead?" I sighed. This was a pet theme of his. Old Indian lies down and wills himself to die, just like in those books of American Indian mysticism he favored. "If only it were that simple. Sorry, I don't think we get out of life that easily. But that's not the point, is it? I'm really beginning to wonder where you're actually going."

Banging the filter against a rock to clear it, he glanced up. "You didn't get my note?"

"Gone to Mexico. Adios?"

He grinned. "Kinda funny, huh?"

"No, it wasn't funny," I said slowly and deliberately. "It was cold and ugly. And hurtful. Again."

His smile slipped a notch. He screwed the filter back together then, bending over, stretched across the rocks and eased it back into the pond.

"And what's with the sneaking away and then back again when I'm not here, well, except for last night? Oh yeah, and what about last night, what the hell was that about?"

"You were on the couch."

I pinched the bridge of my nose between my forefinger and thumb, trying to control the fury that surged up. "Okay, let me get this straight. You left again because I was on the couch?"

"You were supposed to be upstairs in bed."

"Okay, so where did you sleep last night?"

Nudging his glasses up his nose, he pushed against the rocks, rose to his feet with a grunt, and stared thoughtfully down at the pond.

"You slept in the van, didn't you?"

His expression wavered. I was right.

"Wait a minute," I said. "Where's the VW? How did you get home?"

"I got a ride."

"At two in the morning?"

"What do you care?"

"That is so unfair."

"You're giving me a headache."

"*I'm* giving *you* a headache," I shrieked. The back of my neck felt as if a steel rod had been rammed against it. "You take off without a word and I haven't a clue if you're coming back. Have you forgotten I'm supposed to go to South Africa in, what, less than a month? Who's going to take care of the dogs? What about Sweetpea's treatments?"

"I guess you're trapped, then, aren't you?" he said.

"What does that mean? You're leaving again?"

"Maybe."

"What about Sweetpea? I thought you loved her."

"I do." So calm.

"What about the van and the Nomad?" I asked. My eyes blurred.

He shrugged. "Sell 'em."

I gathered up my stuff and charged for the house. "Fuck you!" I cried as I passed him.

Once inside, I fumbled in my purse for my miracle peppermint pills that usually calmed any kind of upset stomach I had. After washing down a pill with bottled water and taking three Advils, I rushed around the house putting things away, trying to calm myself, trying not to throw up.

Ten minutes later, Larry was in the kitchen washing his hands.

"So, let me get this straight," I said, coming up behind him at the sink. "I'm on my own with figuring out what to do with the dogs when I go?"

He didn't turn around. "Guess so."

"Goddam it, don't stonewall me."

"You sure cuss a lot," he said mildly. Without looking at me, he dried his hands on the dishtowel. "Such an angry little woman, aren't you?"

I groaned. "Please don't do this to me."

"Do what?"

Vomit gushed up into my mouth. I charged for the toilet. And so began two nightmarish days spent either in the bathroom or on the couch, where I thrashed around, feverish and shivering. Even my eyelashes hurt. The steel rod at the back of my neck was firmly planted.

Over those two days I was vaguely conscious of Larry's presence. He brought me water, orange juice, an extra blanket. Neither the water nor the orange juice would stay down. The first or second night, I became aware of his feet at the other end of our huge sectional. I resisted the temptation to wrap my legs around his the way I used to.

Three days into the illness, Larry all but carried me into my doctor's office.

I flopped back on the examination table, and the doctor asked a series of questions before examining me.

"I could run a series of tests, but I have a good idea it's viral meningitis," she finally said. "Funny thing, you're the second person I've seen in the last couple of weeks with the same symptoms. And, no, don't worry, I get at least three cases a year. Unlike bacterial meningitis, the viral kind is rarely fatal. Unfortunately, I can't give you anything for it because it is viral. The best thing you can do is rest and drink plenty of fluids. Advil will help. You're healthy, shouldn't take more than a couple of weeks for you to be up and about. If anything changes, let me know immediately."

Ten days later, I was up and ready to walk the dogs. I'd already done some of the laundry, while Larry had done the yard work and grocery shopping. Without my noticing, we had settled back into our old groove, although our relationship was bruised like never before. Despite his customary evasiveness, I got the idea that my guess was right—he had spent the past week with that guy with a house on the beach below Ensenada. That must be where he'd left the VW. Eliciting more information would be too taxing and frustrating, so I left it at that.

With the dogs leading the way, I headed out the back gate. The garage door was open. The 1955 Chevy Nomad we'd purchased twelve years before was pulled slightly forward. Dressed in a grease-stained shirt and shorts, Larry leaned over the engine.

"Putting on more shiny parts?" I asked. Over the years I'd accompanied him to vintage car swap meets to buy chromed parts in an effort to fulfill his goal of "tricking out" the car of his teenage dreams.

He looked up and grinned. "Only seven thousand more to go. To show you how stupid I am, I bought three right door handles and not even one was for the left." He shook his head. "You're right, I am pathetic."

"I've never said you were pathetic."

"Well, you've thought it."

"No, I never thought you were pathetic. Psychotic, yes, but not pathetic."

He grinned. "Keep 'em guessing." He bent back down to his task.

"You're unbelievable."

He grinned. "Hey, where're you going?"

"The hill."

"You're quite the animal, aren't you?"

"Enough lying around."

"You just can't relax, can you?" He bent down to tighten a screw. "I thought the doctor told you to rest."

"I did. Exercise makes me feel better. Hey, listen, about my trip to South Africa."

"Uh-huh," he said from the depths of the engine.

"I'm leaving in a month."

He straightened. "Yeah? I know that. By the way, how *is* your brother?"

"Good, I guess," I said. "You never know with him."

"Well, he didn't say he was sick or anything like that, did he?"

"That's not what's bothering me." I told him my worries about Garth's ability to find new living quarters and my typical frustration and guilt about being so far away.

"You worry too much about everything. You'll find out soon enough how he is. I'm sure you'll handle it, you always do."

I nodded, feeling a little better about the trip.

"Be sure to tell him I said hi next time you talk to him," Larry said.

I recalled our visit to South Africa six years before for my son Layne's wedding. Larry had listened intently to Garth's every word. I recalled the genuine concern in his face, the way he didn't want to leave Garth.

"So now you're going to be here to watch the dogs while I'm gone?"

"Why wouldn't I be?"

"Oh, for God's sake, that isn't what you led me to believe—"

He cocked his head and gave me a half-grin. "You pissed me off with your twenty questions."

I sighed and shook my head. "Games, always games. Why can't you just be straight? I mean on one hand you're supportive, and then you just, just, fuck, I don't know . . ."

He walked out from behind the car and took me in his arms. "Take it easy, take it easy," he said. This was his favorite mantra.

I resisted clinging to him.

"There you are!" a familiar voice cried from behind us.

"How're you doing?" Larry said over my shoulder.

I turned to see a neighbor from down the street, someone we'd known for at least ten years, who—along with her husband—had always joked that trying to pass our house when Larry was out working on his car or playing basketball in the driveway was like trying to get through a vortex. Hours later they'd find themselves on the other side of our house, realizing that they'd just spent hours talking about themselves to a man whose only goal in life, it seemed, was to listen to them. Most of the time they'd turn around and head back home for their cars to complete the task they'd set out to do before they ran into Larry. It was the neighborhood joke.

"Gotta go," I said, allowing the dogs to pull me away. "The hills are a-calling."

"Nice to see you," she called, then said to Larry, "Where *have* you been?"

I hung back to hear what he'd say. "Doin' a little surfing," he said. "And you? How have you guys been?"

She wouldn't learn any more than that, I thought with a sigh. And neither would I. Slipping on my headphones, I headed for the hills, trying not to think about what the future held for us. One day at a time, I told myself. I had my brother's situation to deal with. For now that was more than enough.

Eleven

A WEEK LATER, on a Saturday afternoon, part-time surfing buddy and long-time friend Bob showed up to persuade Larry to go to the wedding of the daughter of an old friend of ours.

"I'll guilt him into it," Bob had told me earlier. I was glad to hear it. Although I intended to go one way or another—maybe hitch a ride with Bob and his wife, who lived in town—I wanted Larry to go as well. I wanted to see how he interacted with others now, especially old friends. Plus, I had some crazy notion that the whole wedding thing would remind him of the vows we'd made, remind him of what we'd had in the beginning.

Bob, Tim, and Joe were three of Larry's oldest friends from the '60s. They, along with their wives, had been my friends, too, for the past twenty-five years. When we received the wedding invitation—this was after his second trip to Mexico—Larry made it clear he wasn't going. "Fuck no" is how he put it. He hated social functions, especially weddings. Still, he always relented, and for the most part ended up enjoying himself. This time, though, he seemed resolved when I pressed him.

"What friends?" he said. "I have no friends."

His standard spiel. He had *acquaintances*, not *friends*, is what he usually said. That way he could distance himself from the emotional currency at the heart of any friendship. The reciprocity, the expectations—the obligations. I didn't get it. I loved my friends. When I accused him of being afraid of getting hurt, said that he was cut off from his emotions, he told me, "Isn't that the goal?"

I'd told Bob about Larry's defections. Bob's response was typical for him: a look of skepticism, like maybe I'd made up these stories about Larry, followed by a selective whittling away at the facts until Larry's actions appeared harmless. I wanted to shake him, but mostly I wanted him to tell me that he thought what Larry was doing was cruel, and that he would take it upon himself to give Larry a thorough talking to. What was I thinking? From what Larry said, they'd never shared anything deeper than surf talk and verbal jousting. I don't think Bob ever even asked Larry about his trips, other than how the surfing had been down in Mexico. But now Bob was determined that Larry go to the wedding, and he made it happen: one six-pack of beer and two basketball games in our driveway later, and we were all going together. I silently cheered. Old times.

I helped Larry set aside his standard attire of shorts/blue jeans, a flannel shirt, and flip-flops, and arranged slightly more formal attire consisting of a pair of dressy grey Levis, a Hawaiian shirt, and huaraches for the ceremony. I was amazed that he acquiesced to my suggestions.

His sisters spoke of him as a clotheshorse in high school and on into his twenties, when his wardrobe had consisted of a dozen pairs of pants with knife-edged pleats he insisted on ironing himself, along with long-sleeved turndown point-collared shirts. I would've liked to have seen that guy. From what I can gather, the change happened with the advent of his first marriage at twenty-three. And then, during the sixties, he grew his black hair into a long ponytail and started wearing peasant-like embroidered shirts, always in the finest fabric. Always elegantly cool.

The wedding ceremony took place in Heisler Park, Laguna Beach, on the lawn on a cliff overlooking the ocean. No expense had been spared. Moments after spotting one another, the four old friends and their wives slipped into that familiar circle of hard hugs and funny banter. Several feet away, I witnessed an exchange between Larry and Pati, Joe's wife.

She was smiling broadly in that animated way of hers and saying, "Don't you just love life and this wonderful day that's been given to us?"

She said things like that. I liked her. I watched in amazement as Larry's face stretched into a phony smile. "Yeah, isn't it great?" he responded, his voice straining with the effort it took.

In the past I would have expected Larry to say something like, "Slow down, Pati." He later told me that she'd enthusiastically declared that the two of them should've been married to each other because, she said, he was so much fun. Joe, witnessing this exchange, rolled his eyes. He didn't seem to take these remarks personally. I didn't. Pati had never made it a secret that she really liked Larry, but she also didn't make it a secret that she liked me, too, and that she thought of me as a kindred spirit. One of the reasons I liked this group of friends was because they knew Larry so well; his off-the-wall comments were expected, freeing me from being his interpreter—or his foil.

"Why on earth would she think I'm fun?" he asked, swiveling around in his seat to face me as he drove us to the reception. He looked puzzled and irritated. An odd question and reaction, given his entertaining persona, the reactions he elicited from women, from people. Before I could answer, he added with a rueful grin, "We both know better, don't we?"

I laughed. "Don't we ever?"

It was only later, at the reception in Tim's backyard, that I realized just how much of a change had taken place in Larry. While the three other couples ragged on each other with well-worn riffs and old grievances, Larry and I were strangely silent. I'd always been able to find something about him to rag on, something he'd done or said, that would elicit laughs and hilarious responses from everyone else; they'd all been at his mercy more than once. He'd always taken it good-naturedly, and then come back with some brilliant zinger.

But this time, a gulf stretched between us. It felt strange not to join in, but I didn't have anything to say about us, about what he'd been doing; everything that had happened in the last eight months had been off the charts, too serious. So I set about enjoying myself instead. Larry kept a smile on his face and made uncharacteristically appropriate remarks. But I could feel his detachment—or maybe "bewilderment" would be a better word for it. Whatever was bothering him had far-reaching effects, and it made me sad.

At the end of the evening, Pati took a photo of the four old friends sitting at the table, heads cocked together, arms draped around each other's shoulders. Larry's smile was forced. Best photo ever, the friends agreed, except for Larry. He remained silent.

Larry and I danced together, slipping into that easy rhythm we'd worked out over the years. He was remote; it was like dancing with a shadow. I also danced with Pati and a couple of guys in a free-for-all on the dance floor. It felt good to be rid of the perplexing drama between Larry and me, at least for a while.

Later, as the party wound down, we all sat around the table in pairs. I heard Larry say to Joe, "I've always wanted to live in my van." I didn't hear Joe's reply. Was he being serious or was he deflecting an uncomfortable question about his defections with an outrageous statement? Probably the latter, but I couldn't help thinking that maybe all my nagging, my demand for answers, as well as his conflicts with his kids—his lack of interest in their lives and irritation over their requests for money—had led him to believe that living in his van, cut off from me, his family, and his kids, was the answer to all his problems.

* * *

The following Monday, Larry asked me to drive him to a body shop in Laguna Niguel to pick up his van where he'd dropped it off a week earlier. Paint was the final step in his overall plan to revamp the '73 relic. It had a new engine and new carpet, the seats had been re-covered, and he'd finally hammered out all the dents and sanded away the rust. When he'd started the process, years before he retired, we'd spoken of taking a road trip to New Mexico and Arizona. I still held out hope that it would happen.

It was one of those warm, summer-like late-fall days that sometimes descend on Southern California. The kind of weather you experience more frequently south of the Mexican border. What had the weather been like all those days and nights Larry had spent down there? I wanted to know more. He was in a good mood, so at the risk of getting pissed off by his evasiveness, I launched right in.

"So did you have your own room at . . . Steve's, was that his name?" I asked.

Half-smiling, Larry slid a wary look in my direction. "Yeah. What did you think?"

"Hell, I didn't know what to think, remember?"

"All right, all right, quit with the twenty questions."

"That was only one and a half questions. Thing is, I still can't see you spending any time with anyone else living within throwing distance. Not to mention being obligated to them for doing so. And doesn't he have a wife? That's two too many people. Doesn't make sense."

"Nothing makes sense in life." He stared out the window.

"Okay, let's not vague out here." I swung the car onto the freeway and glanced at him.

"I was the only one there, if you must know."

"Both times?"

"What? Are you keeping a log?"

"I'm just asking, I mean, what's the big deal?"

"Steve was there for a while. I did some work for him on the place in exchange for staying there."

"What kind of work?"

"What does it matter?"

"I'm just asking," I said.

"I fixed the roof. Okay?"

"Maybe you should build your own little adobe house as an alternative to living in your van."

He shot me a sharp glance. "You shouldn't eavesdrop."

"Did you mean that?"

"Mean what?" he said.

"Living in your van."

"Sounds like fun."

"Honestly? Truly? Really?"

"Kinda. But I'm not quite ready for that." He grinned. "But Joe liked the idea."

"Why do you have to do things like that?" I said.

"Do what?"

"Screw with people."

"It's fun," he said. "Hey, slow down."

"So what's the story?"

"You almost hit that guy." He swung around to look back at a car that had pulled onto the freeway.

"I did no such thing. So, talk to me. You were going to tell me what's been going on with you."

"I was?"

"Dammit!" I turned to glare at him.

"All right, all right, keep your eyes on the road," he said, gripping the dash. A couple of minutes passed before he finally spoke. "It's just that I'm sick of everything here, the crowds, the assholes at the grocery store who run into you with their carts, the jerks who won't let you merge into traffic. Everyone's in a hurry. And surfing sucks. I'm having enough trouble trying to stand up on the board with these little chicken legs of mine without having to fight for a wave. Hell, in the middle of the week it's as crowded as the weekends. Don't these people have jobs?"

This was more than he'd revealed about his escapes before. "So you've been running away, then?"

He snorted. "Running away?"

"Okay, so what do you call it?"

"I told you," he said, an edge of impatience in his voice. "This place has changed. I'm sick of it."

"So why couldn't you have told me all this before?"

"I'm telling you now."

"So what about me?" I swung off the freeway and headed toward the body shop, which was a short distance away.

"What do you mean?"

"You keep taking off out of the blue, no warning, nothing. You act like you're pissed off at me, yet you tell me I've done nothing wrong . . . I mean, we're supposed to be married."

"Yeah?"

"Hey, maybe I'd like to run away too, you know. Why can't we run away *together*?"

He stared out the passenger side window. I waited.

"You've got your job," he said without turning to face me.

"That's it?" I shrieked. "My *job*?"

He turned to face me and frowned. "What do you want me to say?"

The tires screeched as I pulled into the driveway of the body shop. He reached for the door handle. "What's the matter with you?" he said, getting out. "You've got everybody staring at you."

"I want you to tell me the truth," I said.

He got out, shut the door, and bent over to peer in the window at me. He shook his head. "God, you get wound up. I'll see you at home." He turned to go, then doubled back. "Thanks for the ride."

I stared straight ahead, hot tears of frustration stinging my eyes. I should've known better. I was never going to find the right words to make him level with me. I slammed the steering wheel with the heel of my hand. Goddamn him. I couldn't do this anymore. When I got back from South Africa, I would give him an ultimatum: counseling or divorce.

Twelve

LARRY DROPPED ME off curbside at the Los Angeles airport with a quick hug and peck on the cheek. He encouraged me to enjoy myself, told me to say hello to Layne and his family, and Garth and Margaret too, and said that he would pick me up in three weeks. No worries about Sweetpea and Jake, he said. Our breath formed tiny clouds in the cold, pre-dawn air as we said good-bye.

I watched him pull away from the curb with his usual anxiety when merging into traffic, the wildly swiveling head and grateful wave when someone let him in. I could almost see the tips of his fingers, white from strangling the steering wheel. I shook my head. What a bundle of contradictions. Hitching my carry-on bag more firmly onto my shoulder, I turned and hurried into the airport.

I thought about my parting from Sweetpea. Little shit. I've learned to wait until the day before I leave to pack, because the moment she sees my suitcase I'm in for it. First comes the stink eye, then she won't eat, and then that night no sleep for me. Every time I moved to get some air between us in bed, she closed the gap as if I were magnetized. Jake, bless his straight-as-an-arrow little heart, didn't move all night long. Just before leaving, I bent down to give Sweetpea a good-bye kiss in her blue donut bed. She had her nose pressed into the side, eyes barely visible, like a crocodile in the shallows. With every attempt I made, she shifted away,

Sweetpea and the Goodbye Kiss

again and again, until she'd spun completely around.

I finally stretched out beside her on the floor and bit her muscled cheek. She ignored me. I bit the tip of her ear. Her head came up and she swung around. I grabbed her head between my hands and kissed her full on her snout. She hung there for a moment, pressed into the kiss. Then I gently lowered her head back down and she settled into the side of her bed with a loud, satisfied groan.

"I love you, baby girl," I whispered. "I'll be back." She glanced up at me for a long moment before settling back into being a crocodile. Jake panted and paced, then followed me to the door, his dark eyes stretched wide with a burning question: *Can I come with you?* I grabbed his ears, kissed him hard between the eyes, and left.

It was the usual flight from hell. Twenty-four hours of cramped, crazy legs and the nerve-racking dirge of throbbing engines. And, on top of that, my usual dread at the prospect of going home. This was only the fourth time I'd ventured back in thirty-seven years. The first time had been shortly after my dad died in 1974; then with Larry and Darin when Layne got married the first time in 1996; and then again when he married Irma two years prior. Now this.

I loved Africa. I hated it. For ten years after I emigrated to America, I had this recurring nightmare in which I was back in the Northern Rhodesian bush, charging down Ndola airport's runway, waving and screaming after a plane that had taken off without me, leaving me stuck back there forever. Stuck with trying to reconcile the casual, everyday tragedies of life: the injustices, the beatings and killings—of humans and animals. I would be stuck in a pitiless and stifling way of life devoid of imagination and inspiration. Stuck with a future of organizing the servants, having babies, and indulging in an endless round of "sundowners"—five o'clock cocktail time—and affairs in Nkana, "hub" of the Copperbelt. It chafed at my soul and made me desperate for something more.

Shortly after I married John, I drove all the way to Lusaka, capital of Northern Rhodesia, to apply for a visa to emigrate to the States. John wanted to head south to Southern Rhodesia to buy a tobacco farm with his parents. This was when the country was the "bread basket" of Africa—before it became Zimbabwe, before Robert Mugabe took over and eventually trashed the country, betraying his own people in his megalomania. But before any plans were made to buy the farm and before the visa came through, John accidentally killed a black policeman.

The man was drunk, staggering down the middle of Central Street. We were on our way home from a party at Mindola Dam in our 1964 Mini Cooper. It was a black hole of a night, sheets of rain engulfing the little Cooper. The man flew over the bonnet, bounced on the Mini's roof, and landed on the road ten feet to the left of the car. The car's roof caved in on top of my head, knocking me out.

When I came to, lights pulsed in my head, along with an image of that woman's car that had been firebombed on the road to Ndola when she stopped at an intersection. Africans had thrown a Molotov cocktail through the window and then beaten her and her two children to death as they crawled from their blazing car.

Hands wrenched open the Mini's door and reached for me. John stood staring helplessly down at the policeman's body in the headlights. For two agonizing hours at Nkana Mine hospital, a no-nonsense British nurse plucked shards of windshield glass from my forearms and hands with tweezers. I spent the night with a suspected concussion, my hands and arms bandaged. John had a few cuts.

The white colonial court of Northern Rhodesia still in charge at the time ruled it an accident. The policeman was drunk and staggering down the middle of the street in the middle of the night in a blinding storm. We didn't see him. End of story. A little while later, a white lawyer working for United National Independence Party, the ruling political party, took the case to seek true justice for the people of the new country of Zambia—some said it was a political move. So much for John's tobacco farm. Two weeks before the trial we fled with Darin to America along with eighty-eight pounds of luggage and a student visa. I would finally make it to the country of my dreams, albeit under a dark cloud.

Now I looked out the airplane window. "Welcome to Oliver Tambo International Airport," a South African woman's voice droned over the intercom. "Where the temperature is 35 degrees Celsius, 95 degrees Fahrenheit." I'd forgotten that South Africa's eleven-year-old fledgling black regime had renamed the airport after a key anti-apartheid figure, replacing the familiar name of the former Prime Minister, Jan Smuts. So much change—change I'd never dreamed possible. The radical kind of change I needed to make in my own life.

After a smartly uniformed African—a woman, no less—waved me through Customs, I headed for baggage pickup, a long, scarred, and groaning conveyor belt that emerged from behind a curtain of dangling, licorice-like rubber strips. Half an hour later, my luggage finally appeared. I caught a glimpse behind the scenes of an army of shoulder-to-shoulder Africans in blue overalls passing luggage onto the conveyor belt from a truck. A couple of workers probably could've done the job, but the government's plan was to employ as many Africans as possible—albeit at lower rates—in a plan to fulfill campaign promises and combat the highest violent crime rate in the world. A couple of these same workers lounged against one of the posts. I thought back to the days when this same attitude elicited a cuff behind the ear and a comment about lazy *kaffirs*.

Layne, seven-year-old Daegan, his wife Irma, and her two daughters, thirteen-year-old Illanka and fifteen-year-old Bianca, rushed forward from a sea of faces to greet me. A real airport pickup. Not like Larry's usual drive-bys. I was home with people who valued me. After the typical, South African–style body-crushing hugs and full on kisses on the mouth, we piled into Irma's Mercedes SUV. With a torrent of apologies in Afrikaans—yes, my son had married an Afrikaaner—for the slightest transgressions in true South African fashion, the girls followed me onto the backseat. Daegan piled into the rear compartment.

We headed toward Centurion, where they owned a house in a gated community. The highway, which consisted of twin, two-lane strips of tarmac, stretched across the savanna. Nothing like the concrete jungles I'd grown accustomed to in the States. But here, too, there was traffic. Lots of it. More than I remembered. Cars that looked vaguely familiar, variations of the models found in America but with unfamiliar names, and lots of bakkies—pickup trucks. The bushveld still had the familiar profile of my memories: concrete, pinch-waisted grain silos, linked at top with a bar, and plateaus of finely crushed rock—mine workings from the birth of South Africa's first gold mining operations in 1886—some of them one hundred and sixty-four feet high, most covered in grass and shrubs.

Having grown up in the Northern Rhodesian "bush," South Africa was the big time when I was a kid. I had to be on my best behavior and wear shoes every time we visited our relatives, twelve hundred miles away. The funny thing is, while the spacious mine houses up in Nkana had indoor toilets, my Uncle Len and Aunt Ivy's Johannesburg toilet was outside, a chilly trek down steep narrow stairs in what in England would be called a council house, where the wind blew up your bottom on those cold June winter months.

Fifteen miles east lay Pretoria, the capital, where my grandparents used to live on a jacaranda-lined street in a three-bedroom house near the houses of Parliament. What would my stern, London-born grandfather say about today's South Africa—of having to live in a house surrounded by electrified barbed wire to keep out robbers who, before apartheid, didn't dare be caught on the streets after dark?

Beyond was Roodepoort, town of my birth: forty miles and a lifetime away. I have no memory of the place beyond a black-and-white photo of me at fourteen months old with my dad and one of his bantams. According to my dad, I loved to drop the chickens' eggs in their water bowl, much to his delight. My father's wild child. Perhaps it was things like this that drew my grandfather's ire. Or was it my mother always telling him how impossible I was? Regardless, I didn't fit in with the rest of the cousins. I didn't belong: I was the bush kid.

This was ten years after World War II, when anyone in South Africa with extra pigment in their skin or who looked different in any way was considered a second-class citizen. Lucky for me, mine was a white bloodline: Scottish on my Dad's side, English through my mother's stiff-necked father. And German and French through my sweet grandma, whose family had come to South Africa at the beginning of the nineteenth century.

We were considered "English" South Africans, as opposed to the Afrikaaners, because our primary bloodline was English and we spoke English at home. Afrikaaners spoke Afrikaans—a combination of Flemish and Dutch that, after a 1925 act of Parliament, replaced standard Dutch as one of the two official languages of the Union of South Africa.

The almost three years I spent in South Africa from age seven to ten—this was after the eighteen months of isolation in Southern Rhodesia, when my dad managed Mr. Bradley's sisal estate—were harrowing. I had to learn Afrikaans and sometimes dodge bullying Afrikaaner boys looking for *roinek* blood. The term, meaning "red neck," was a holdover from the Boer War, when the Boers supposedly could pick off British soldiers in the distance solely by the sight of their tender English necks burnt bright red by the brutal South African sun.

Now I turned to see Bianca shoving coins into the hands of two ragged white children, who couldn't be more than eight or ten, standing beside a stop sign.

"Shame," Irma said, turning around to watch them. "Poor kids. This is the second time I've seen them here." She relayed the story of how their father had abandoned them after their mother died. "And then last week," she continued, "I read in the newspaper about a homeless white community in Bethlehem. The headline read, 'One Million of SA's three-million Afrikaaners Are Destitute, Homeless.'"

"Really?"

"Honestly. The fastest-growing segment of our society. They haven't quite caught up to the blacks yet, though. It's all very sad. We do what we can for all of them with our Rand at stop signs. There is no other way."

"That's awful," I said, turning to look back at the children. "Equal opportunity poverty."

"Hey Mom," my son said, glancing in the rearview mirror at me. He swung onto the Centurion off-ramp and pointed at a sign that showed a line through a running figure. "You'll like this one."

"No running off the freeway?" I said.

"No carjacking."

I laughed. "Now that's funny. Does it work?"

"It does. This used to be the number one spot. The carjackers would hide in that big clump of bushes and jump out as people came to a stop."

"And the sign did it?"

"Uh, huh. 'Course the hijackers just moved operations to another spot."

"Another sign?"

"There's quite a few of them around."

"We're an obedient bunch, aren't we?" I said. "What is it about us South Africans, black or white? Give us a directive and we snap to attention. Of course, killing and mayhem can take place at the drop of a hat, but there is something about following rules, isn't there?" I caught Layne's eye in the rearview mirror and grinned at him. "Well, except for you, my sweet. But then, you were born in America."

He laughed.

"It's true," Irma said. "He gets away with murder."

"Just like—"

Me and Dad with Bantam

"My stepdad," Layne cut in with a laugh.

"I was going to say just like my dad, but yeah, just like him." I tried to keep my voice even.

"How is the old dog?" Layne said. "Damn, you should've *made* him come with you."

"He's good, but he had to take care of Sweetpea, the whole dialysis thing, you know? And Jake, of course." I glanced out the window. Despite myself, I missed Larry being here with us. But I couldn't tell them about his defections. "So what's going on with Garth?"

"Tell your mom about his SMSs," Irma said.

"SMSs?" I said.

"Instant messages," Irma said. "They're huge here."

"Garth?"

"He signed up with some site that sends out SMSs," Layne said. "Some kind of solicitation, actually, I'm not exactly sure how it works."

"How did he find out how to do that?"

"The man is full of surprises," Layne said. "He probably saw something on TV."

"Well, he did go down to 'the television shop' that time his was stolen, remember?" I said. "And they gave him another TV."

"I'd love to know what really happened there," Layne said.

"'I needed another TV' is all I could get out of him. And that funny little smile when you're asking questions that confuse him," I said.

"*Being There*," Irma said.

"Beg your pardon?" I said.

"Peter Sellers as Chauncey Gardner in that movie where he walks on water because he doesn't realize he can't," Irma said.

"I like that," I said, smiling at her. Garth walking on water? Maybe I hadn't failed him after all.

"Back to the SMSs," Layne said. "One day, I get this message on my phone saying something like, 'Hey there sexy, let's get together for a drink.' And then another, 'I think we would make a great couple, can I call you sometime?' They were general pickup messages. I didn't know where they were coming from, until one came with some message like, 'If you want to get together then phone me at this particular number.' It's Garth's cell phone number. So I call him and ask him if he's been sending me SMSs. He says yes, he has, but he's a little hesitant, like he's thinking he's done something wrong."

"Poor Garth," I said.

"Mom, I can hear that tone in your voice, don't spaz out on me, here," Layne said, catching my eyes in the rearview mirror. "I'm the only one he sent the messages to, I'm pretty sure. I don't think he actually knew what was in them. He probably just pressed one of the selections. Anyway, they stopped."

"Well, you've got to hand it to him," I said. "He's trying new things."

"You really must give him credit for other things as well," Layne said. "He's taken care of not only himself but Margaret for the past, how long as it been, twenty years or so?"

"Twenty-five," I murmured.

"Would you have had the money to pay for all his medications for the rest of his life?" Layne continued. "To cover the cost of health care in the States with someone who's uninsurable? And then what would become of him if something happened to you? He'd be stranded in the States."

"Yeah, but look how he's living now," I said.

"We don't know for sure how he's living now," Layne said. "Besides, he'll be moving soon. We'll sort everything out when we get down to Durban, okay?"

"Did I ever tell you about the time I took Garth to the Astra?" I asked—then stopped. The memory wasn't a good one. What had prompted me to tell them this story, a desire for self-flagellation? "Never mind, you don't want to hear it."

"Oh, no you don't," Layne said. "I haven't heard this one before."

"I want to hear your story, Granny Sandra," Daegan said.

"It's actually kind of embarrassing."

"All the better to hear," Layne said.

"Oh, what the hell. Long, long ago, when I was fifteen and Garth was seven, we had these two 'bioscopes' in Nkana—that's what we called movie theaters. The Astra was in the town part of our little bush world. The Rhokana Cinema was up near the mines, opposite the Mine Club, the part of town owned by the mining company. Saturday matinees were a big deal. My girlfriends and I got to check out the 'talent' and they got to check us out in our big petticoats and belt-cinched, eighteen-inch waists.

"So, Garth had been begging me for years to take him to the Astra. I was so afraid he'd do something stupid—talk too loud, take forever to answer a question, pick his nose in public . . ." I trailed off, sorry I'd started the story.

"Go on," Irma and the two girls said in unison.

I sighed. "Okay, so, on this particular day, my mother had enough of Garth's begging, so that was that. I took all the back lanes, dragging him along, and I waited until the picture had started before sneaking in. I prayed the seats in the back near the door were vacant. They were. So as "God Save the Queen" wound down and everyone was still standing at attention, we slipped into the two seats right by the entrance. I glanced toward the section where my friends usually sat, but what with all the cigarette smoke and the lights dimming, I couldn't tell who was there.

"Garth's eyes were glued to the screen, his mouth hanging open. Please, God, don't let him do anything stupid, I'm thinking. After the previews of coming attractions, *Seven Brides for Seven Brothers* came on. I *loved* that movie. All that dancing. I was so glad it wasn't a cowboy and Indian movie. Whenever my parents took us to one of those, Garth always went nuts, jumping up and down and yelling, or clapping like mad. After a while, I forgot about him. And then the unthinkable happened. I hadn't even noticed, but he'd climbed up onto his seat and started jumping up and down—and all of a sudden the seat slammed back and he was stuck. I almost passed out. This couldn't be happening.

"He starts struggling like he's trapped in the jaws of a crocodile and yelling like a madman. I hunch over, hoping no one will see it's me, and grab him by the thigh and yank up, first one then the other. But nothing's happening. Every eye in the place is on us. I can feel it. We're the show. I stand, grab him under the armpits, and jerk him up. He yells even louder. I just keep yanking. I don't remember how I got him out. It felt like hours later, but it couldn't have been more than a couple of minutes. There's this gash on his leg, blood's trickling down into his sock. He's sobbing." I stopped, overcome by the memory. Truth is, I smacked him on the arm in my panic. That's when he stopped yelling and started crying. The look on his face.

"And then what happened?" Daegan said.

I couldn't remember what happened next, and yet, looking around the car, I felt that I had to put a happy twist on the ending. Hooking my arm around Daegan's neck, I said, "I told Garth I was so terribly sorry and that I'd get him an ice cream sandwich later. He happily agreed and went back to watching the show." I probably did promise Garth some sweet, some favor, to make him stop crying, but I wasn't sure. What I did know for certain was that the incident was seared into my heart. I wondered if Garth even remembered what happened that day—and if he did, I wondered if he remembered any wrongdoing on my part. I doubted it. In his eyes I could do no wrong.

"Well, here's our lovely little compound," Layne said, drawing up to a guard shack and a post with a gate. The sun, which was dipping behind a hill, oozed crimson and gold across the sky. Layne slid his card into a slot; the gate swung up and we drove through. Two smartly uniformed Africans waved as we passed.

"That's it on security?" I asked.

"Works most of the time," Irma said. "It helps to have dogs."

None of the houses in the three-acre development were more than ten years old, and they all favored a Tuscany style. The yards, smaller than those of my youth, were walled rather than hedge-enclosed, and there were hardly any trees. The foliage, though, was the same as ever: red, yellow, white, and purple gladioli as big as my fist; magenta, orange, and white bougainvillea blooms the size of teacups; and lawns on steroids, all of it seeming to grow as you watched.

That night, Layne treated me to a good old South African braaivleis—literal translation "roast meat"—along with my beloved gem squash and *sadza*, that thickened cornmeal I'd shared with Leffy beside his fire. Irma and I slipped back into the warm, sisterly relationship we'd established upon first meeting two years earlier. Later, we opted to sit on the back verandah instead of watching the movie *Cars* with the rest of the family.

"Look at that," Irma said, grinning. She inclined her head toward the living room.

Sprawled on the couch were fifteen-year-old Bianca and eight-year-old Daegan, snuggled on either side of Layne. Illanka stood behind the couch, rubber banding Layne's hair into a forest of short blond tufts, except for two pink clips in front. I jumped up and grabbed my camera. Layne grinned as I took the shot. Illanka giggled and jumped out of the way. All I got of her was one long, tanned leg.

Smiling, I returned to my seat. "I never got a real chance to see him interact with the girls when you two got married. I'm sure he told you how important family is to him, and that that's why he came to South Africa—to connect with as many members of our family as he could, to be surrounded by family. I never realized how much he'd missed having an extended family growing up. Of course, none of his grandparents are around anymore, and there are just a few cousins on John's side, so this is just . . ." I broke off, feeling my throat close.

"He's the best father in the world," Irma said. "I love it. Especially since their own dad hasn't been there for them."

We settled into a comfortable silence.

* * *

Two days after I landed in South Africa, Larry still hadn't called. I knew if I called him, I'd just be snarky. That ever-hopeful expectation that he was going to come around. I wondered how Sweetpea was doing, but no worries there. If something had happened to her, he would call me. So I tried to block him out of my mind and threw myself into the family's activities: grocery shopping and trips to the mall with the girls, who kept buying me little mementos; family dinners that involved linking hands around the table to give thanks for the food and for family, along with Layne's added gratitude for having his mom back. And then there were those spontaneous hugs from Daegan. I felt like some kind of orphan who'd hit the jackpot. It seemed my eyes were constantly brimming with tears—was I turning into a sappy fool? Yet at the same time, I felt like a phony. I couldn't be honest about Larry. I was already growing tired of giving mealy-mouthed answers for what would've normally turned into hilarious riffs about the old days.

That night, after Layne's dinner of lamb curry and rice, Daegan, Layne, the girls, and their two Labradors headed for the swimming pool. Irma excused herself to catch up on some chores. I called Garth to tell him we'd see him in a couple of days. I ended up shouting into the phone; his hearing had definitely become worse. One more thing the poor man had to deal with. The thought put me in a funk. I took my glass of wine and headed for the pool.

Slumping into a chair, I waved to the jumping, shouting, and splashing mass of bodies and fur in and around the kidney-shaped pool. Then I propped my feet on the chair in front of me and laid my head back. Would I ever resolve the guilt that I hadn't taken charge of Garth's life when our parents died? I stared up at clouds that can only be seen in Africa, impossibly large vapors that seem to have floated in from another universe. To my left, in the direction of the airport, a sheet of rain extended down from a load of grey.

Had it rained the day Garth was born? No. It had been a sunny afternoon. Full of promise. I couldn't wait for the baby brother who would be my companion, my ally. I had turned eight the month before, and because we'd moved around a number of times—from Nkana to an isolated sisal plantation in Zimbabwe to various mines in South Africa and then back to Nkana—I spent much of my time alone. I couldn't wait to play doll with him, to dress him up and change his nappy. Only that didn't happen. He was too sick, too fragile. All those allergies that restricted everything he did, and the enlarged heart that made him tired. He would defy the odds that he wouldn't live past his twenties, but at the time my mother was devastated. She'd already lost two sons before me in risky pregnancies—I popped out like a grape—and now that she'd had a son at last, the one who would be her "little man," he was sick.

But worst of all was when my parents learned that five-year-old Garth was "retarded," as they called it back then. The prognosis was that he would forever have the mind of a five-year-old. My dad was stunned at first but then seemed resigned, except that his admonitions for me not to upset my mother grew more urgent. She became fretful and weepy when drunk, staring at Garth with anguished eyes. She doted on him, indulging his every whim. They both did. That was my dad's way with both of us.

Over the years I'd hear her mention her "nervous breakdowns." I don't remember any particular incidents, but I'm sure she must've been in emotional turmoil for a long time after Garth was born. Once, when she seemed to be more upset than usual—and she'd been drinking—I overheard her moan to her girlfriend, "Why did it have to be him?"

Why wasn't I the sick one? Healthy, wild child me, not Garth? Maybe I heard it wrong. Maybe I imagined that conversation. All I know is that I always felt she loved him more than she did me.

Suddenly Layne was behind me; he scooped me up in his arms and ran toward the pool. I struggled to get away and he almost dropped me. I grabbed him around the neck just as he jumped into the pool. "You little turd," I gasped as we hit the water.

"You looked way too serious, Mum."

Thirteen

WE LEFT FOR Durban two days later in the SUV: Layne and Irma up front, me, Illanka, and Bianca in back, and Daegan in the space behind us. They were all looking forward to the holiday Durban afforded—dream town of my youth, stuck as I had been in landlocked Zambia. I was a mess, filled with feelings of love and futility and fear at what I'd find. I'd be doing a lot of journal-writing about this visit, I thought.

At 5 p.m. we arrived at the flat Layne had rented in Shaka's Rock, a beach community north of Durban. "Malibu," the sign proclaimed as we drove up to the guard shack in front of an enclosed two-acre area sporting a clubhouse, swimming pool, miles of lawn, and at least seventy two-story brick condos.

"Welcome to Mellyboo," said the black uniformed guard, touching his fingers to his cap.

The flat was bigger than my Hobbit house back in Laguna Beach: four bedrooms and a deck with a view that took in banana trees, creeping vines, and the lush, verdant foliage typical of the coast of KwaZulu, as well as a sweeping panorama of the foam-edged cerulean blue waters of the Indian Ocean. Everything seemed to drip with humidity.

It was arranged that we would pick up Garth and Margaret in the arcade on the ground floor of their London House flat at 11:00 a.m. the following morning, spend the day at the beach, and then come back to Shaka's Rock for dinner.

It had been a shock to me when I first discovered that my little brother had moved into a flat on the ninth floor of a ten-story building that sat above a shopping arcade on Durban's busy main drag, West Street.

The two of us had never lived in anything other than three- or four-bedroom houses in mining communities, except for on the sisal plantation in Southern Rhodesia, where we lived under a corrugated tin roof in a house that ran on a generator.

After my father died of a heart attack at sixty-five in Kimberley hospital—he was still working on the diamond mines—my mother and Garth moved to the small Coogee Beach Hotel two blocks from Durban's main beach. I always wondered if my mother had been the one to decide to live at the Coogee. I never asked her. I couldn't imagine it. She'd never even learned to drive. My dad had probably arranged it all before his death. He would've made sure that the two of them lived comfortably, if modestly, by the sea for the rest of their lives, a huge luxury for mining types. But five years later my mother died, and Garth stayed on by himself for two years with Coogee's African maids keeping a motherly eye on him until the hotel changed hands and underwent an expensive renovation, forcing him out.

Around the same time, Margaret, a handicapped woman eight years Garth's senior with whom he worked at a government-sponsored company on the outskirts of Durban that made chairs and tables, offered to share her flat with him. At first I thought Margaret also had mental disabilities, but then I realized that she was probably just reticent and/or shell-shocked from life's blows: a crushed pelvis thirty-five years ago when her then-husband floored his truck and backed over her as she stood in the driveway trying to stop him from leaving. I'd only learned about this a couple of years prior in a brief, matter-of-fact account from Margaret herself. When I first met her she was on crutches and wore some kind of leg brace that forced her to shift stiff-legged from side to side in order to walk, but that became too painful, so now she was confined to a wheelchair.

In the beginning, Garth referred to her as his girlfriend. I was so glad to hear this, but I finally realized that sharing a flat was for her a matter of expediency. She needed help with the rent and getting around after her mother died. I don't think she led him on. I think it was Garth's simplistic view of the world: if a girl hangs out with a boy, then she must be his girlfriend. There was also a sister in the picture who lived in Hillary, fifteen miles from Durban. Margaret spent the weekend with her now and then. I pieced all this together over the years; neither Garth nor Margaret said much about anything, other than "Please send more Cheetos."

The following morning, with everyone packed into the SUV, we headed for Durban as planned. A swarm of butterflies had taken residence in the pit of my stomach.

"JAP Cars—Cheap!" The sign on an eight by eight-foot billboard came into view as we crested the hill.

"*Jap* cars?" I said. "Yow!"

"Don't you have Jap cars in America then, hey, Granny Sandra?" Daegan asked, shooting over the back of the seat, close enough to stare cross-eyed at me.

"Um, yes we do. Lots of them. It's the word 'Jap,' m'love. It's a bad word in the States, like the word *kaffir* was, is, over here. It happened after World War II began, when the Americans weren't being nice to the Japanese who lived in America."

"So must I not say Jap, then?" Daegan asked.

"Uh, Irma, Layne, help," I said.

"It has absolutely no connotation here, Mom," Layne said. "Hey, Daegs, just don't say it when you go to America, okay? You don't want to hurt anyone's feelings."

"I won't," Daegan said firmly.

I grabbed him around the neck and kissed him hard on the side of his head. "And you will probably remember to do just that."

Mister Sensitive, unlike Larry, who loved to stir things up, politically correct or not. Damn. The man was never far from my thoughts.

Parking was a bitch on the strip of West Street where London House was located, so Layne tripled-parked while I dodged a barrage of South African–style taxis: barely road-worthy minibuses with music pumping and a couple of black arms sticking out of the windows, making hand gestures to indicate whether seats were available and in which direction

the minibus was headed. A culture shock for me. The only buses I remembered had been filled with white faces and only a couple of black
or Indian ones in the back.

I almost didn't see the shabbily dressed little old man and over-
weight woman in the wheelchair near the edge of the curb. If they hadn't
been white, I might've missed them in the crowds swirling around them.
Garth? Margaret? I tried not to freak out at the decrepit, bazaar-like atmosphere of the arcade, a far cry from the modest (if slightly run-down)
building where I'd last visited Garth in 1996.

Pasting on a smile, I gave them both a hug and pointed toward
Layne's SUV. As always, I had forgotten how small my brother was.
We're the same height—5'2"—but he looks smaller. Layne folded Mar-
garet's wheelchair into the back and loaded her and Garth into the SUV.
Daegan climbed onto Garth's lap.

After a quick enquiry as to Margaret and Garth's health and
well-being—"Fine," they both said—Layne gave a whoop and merged
back into traffic. Irma scrabbled for his sunglasses as they slid across the
dashboard. Daegan cheered; Illanka and Bianca rolled their eyes, but
with that sparkle reserved just for him. Garth, peering around Daegan,
grinned with delight. Daegan turned and smiled at Garth and Margaret.

"Isn't my dad funny?"

Garth nodded, his smile broadening.

"Has anybody ever given you any trouble, Garth?" I said. "You
know, like somebody being nasty to you or Margaret?"

He looked at me for a long moment, as if trying to process my
question. "Not really."

"So people have *sort of* been nasty then?"

"No, I don't think so."

"Like when you ride the bus or eat over at Wimpy or at the shops,
you know, stuff like that?"

He slowly shook his head.

I turned to Margaret. "Have they?"

She shrugged and smiled.

"You're doing okay then, hey Margaret?" I said feeling a sense of
futility. Would I ever know what went on in their lives? What were the
right questions to ask?

She shrugged again. "They made me retire because I can't get around anymore. Those bloody braces hurt too much."

"Except that time they stole my TV," Garth said. "And then that other time, my tape recorder."

"I'm telling you, it was that bloody bloke from work," Margaret said.

"Did you report it?" I asked.

"Report it?" Garth said.

"To the police," I said.

He let out a nervous giggle, like I'd asked him a really hard question to which he didn't know the answer.

"It was old stuff," Margaret said.

I nodded. At least he'd gotten the TV replaced. "So you've got another place lined up, then? I must tell you, London House looks like hell."

"The fuses keep blowing," Garth said. "And the bloody lift always breaks."

"That was very clever of you to find another place," I said. "What's the name of it?"

"The Somerset," Garth said. "I put my name down again."

"Again?"

"Ja."

"Margaret?" I said.

"It was full for July."

"So when—" I began.

"Hey, Mom, we'll sort everything out later, okay?" Layne said. "Today we're just going to have fun."

"Good idea," I said. "Let's have us some fun."

Fourteen

WHEN I WAS fourteen, my parents and me and my whiny little brother finally arrived in Durban after driving twelve hundred miles from Nkana. We had traveled over narrow, partially tarred roads through tsetse fly country, dodging leaping bucks and owls snoozing in the middle of the road. We stopped only to do our business in the bush, using a stack of scratchy toilet paper sheets my mom had brought along. Sometimes somebody kept cavey, on guard, for snakes; sometimes not.

The exhilarating aroma of brine, seaweed, and candy floss—that air-spun, sugary pink confection sold on the boardwalk—enveloped me as we came within sight of the ocean. I waited until my parents were pouring their first holiday drink into the hotel's stubby glasses, a small gin and water to chase away the dust and ache of the drive, before I shot out the door—"Get back here, missy!" yelled my mother. Barefoot and still dressed in my grubby shorts and blouse, I charged down West Street toward Marine Parade, and beyond that the beach. Like a flock of exotic birds, sinewy Zulu men covered in layers of intricately beaded and tasseled vests and aprons, quills and feather boas, along with animal hair leggings, trailed their garish, large-wheeled rickshaw carts up and down

Marine Parade. Others lolled against their carts waiting for customers. Each one of them wore an outrageous headdress as tall as they were. From a simple pair of horns, the diadems grew into tottering giants with four painted horns and vast beaded displays worthy of Rio's Carnaval. Every now and then, those with a full load of passengers would shoot into the air with a shriek and pedal wildly in the air; the cart would tip back, almost touching the ground, and their passengers would squeal with delight.

There were the usual "Whites Only" signs posted in English and Afrikaans on benches, at the wading pool, and by the toilets. Indian peddlers strolled up and down the beach hawking African-made bead necklaces and bracelets and candy floss on trays strung around their necks in loud sing-song voices. Durban has had a substantial Indian population since the mid-nineteenth century, when the British began shipping them to South Africa as indentured laborers to work on the sugar plantations on the coast around Durban, or in the coal mines further inland.

All I was interested in was the Pavilion, a huge, blue, observatory-like building on the boardwalk where they held dances. This had been the capital of my budding teenage fantasy world ever since I'd seen that banner on the top floor advertising some dance event the year before. This time it was Dickie Loader and The Blue Jeans. I ached to dance. Sometimes my dad drove me to the dance "sessions" at the O.B. Bennett Hall or the Anglican Church and picked me up two hours later, filling the doorway with his presence. During my juvenile delinquent years, me and my girlfriends concocted elaborate plans involving lying and scheming to get rides to the five other Copperbelt towns to dance at the sessions there.

But here in Durban, I wasn't allowed to go to the Pavilion—not the year before, and not this time. My dad wasn't about to let me out of his sight; all boys were bastards was what he said, especially city boys. And I certainly didn't want him glaring at every boy who approached me, so I didn't push it.

Two years later, when I was sixteen, Dickie Loader and The Blue Jeans came to Nkana. You would have sworn they were some kind of American rock stars the way we all went berserk for them. Dickie fell for my friend Scarlett, she with the "snake eyes"—breasts larger than the rest of us. Don't ask me how the duck-tailed, sixteen-year-old boys of Nkana came up with a term like "snake eyes" for big breasts. But we figured that was the only reason Dickie chose her and not one of us.

* * *

Layne parked three blocks from the ocean. Once Margaret was settled in the wheelchair, we headed toward the boardwalk. Irma and I took turns with Layne pushing Margaret down West Street. Unlike years ago, when it was lined with white-owned dress and trinket shops, West Street was now crammed with Indian shops selling saris and bunny chow—a delicious, hollowed-out round of bread filled with lamb curry.

I scanned the side streets for the Palmerston Hotel. This is where we stayed on our Durban trips those millions of years ago, and where I met Mr. Jones the year I was twelve. Tall and square-jawed, he smoked a pipe and looked a little like Gregory Peck. He was probably in his mid-sixties. He had retired from the South African Navy and lived in the Palmerston.

We went for walks down to the harbor, where he told me about the ships and the navy and his son, who was also in the navy. It was all pretty much over my head, but he was kind and attentive and sometimes bought me an ice cream. One day he took me to a bookstore and bought me *The Scarlet Pimpernel*. This was a sign that he took me seriously. Even though it was difficult, I read the book all the way to the end, probably because he'd told me I was smart and needed to start reading books like that.

When I got home, I wrote a letter inviting him to come and live with us. He could take the train from Durban up to Nkana, a three-day trip, and he could have Garth's room. I'd let Garth share mine. I even figured that he should come for Christmas, when my mother decorated the house with colored crepe paper chains that she laboriously cut and put together over several days. I told my dad about my plan in the car on our way to mail the letter. He was incredulous at first, and then, like he always did whenever I shared one of my crazy plans with him, spluttered and kept throwing out reasons why it wouldn't work: Garth's room was too small, what would Mr. Jones do all day, what about his family, how would he get around? I had an answer for each one of the obstacles. Finally, he turned to me in exasperation, and said, "Dammit, no. Okay?" I tore up the letter and sulked for two days, but Mr. Jones and I kept up a correspondence for two years, until his letters stopped. I looked for him the next time we went to Durban, but he had disappeared.

And now it occurred to me that the small, somber, three-story building tucked into a narrow street to my left was the Palmerston Hotel.

"Go ahead," I told everyone. "I've got to take a quick charge down memory lane." I hurried toward the hotel.

A burly white man in a dark blue suit, white shirt, tie, and scuffed black shoes stood impassively in the corner of the reception area, his hands folded over his barrel-belly. Security, I realized with a start; I was still not used to this new, lawless South Africa. Otherwise, it looked like it might be the same old lobby. At least the counter was still in the same place. But hadn't there been more brass accents before?

I saw my parents doing the fox-trot on the Palmerston's small dance floor in the lounge. Elbows out and linked at the waist, they glided and dipped across the floor, my dad's fingers pressed into the small of my mother's back, her head tipped back and cocked ever so slightly to the right, dimples flashing. They were hot together on the dance floor, in sync for once. A tide of nostalgia crashed over me, leaving me weepy and trembling. Turning on my heel, I hurried back to where I'd left everybody.

"Are you all right, San?" my brother asked.

"Do you remember the Palmerston?" I asked in a voice thick with tears, regretting the question immediately. I didn't want to remember any more than I had.

He smiled blankly.

"Good," I said, linking my arm through his, relief flooding me. He didn't question me. He never did.

With Daegan and Illanka trailing behind, we all crossed Marine Parade and headed for the beach. I almost didn't see the knot of rickshaw boys in front of the Aquarium. Lolling against their carts, they were lost in throngs of tourists and curio-selling natives with their wares spread down the sidewalk. Had the men always been so scrawny? And what was with the occasional plastic vest? I remembered them as tall, proud Zulus who, calling to the tourists with whistles and shouts, took up half the block with their rickshaws. Now there were only a handful of them. And were they even Zulu?

To our left, hordes of black schoolchildren decked out in neatly pressed green uniforms, white socks, and black shoes spilled out of two buses and ran past us onto the sand, where they would have to fight for space on the beach jammed with black bodies. The sea roiled with African children. No Indians hawking jewelry, not one white sunbather in sight. The whites, used to having elbow room and order on the beach, stayed away from this new, unruly crowd that had no problem with squeezing thigh to thigh, with stumbling over each other. Plus there were still those of the old school, like my Uncle Percy, who retained the apartheid mindset.

Groups of tourists, mostly white, strolled along the boardwalk.

I looked for the Pavilion. Even that looked smaller. And it wasn't blue anymore. The trinket shops below had been replaced by coffee and bikini shops and Wimpy Burgers. If not for the Wimpy, I could've been in Southern California.

"Hey, Mum, come quickly, get in the photo," Layne called. I turned to see Irma, Garth, Daegan, and the girls grouped around Margaret's wheelchair, all of them barely visible through a blur of pigeon wings. Bits of dried corn disappeared from the kids' upturned palms, along with yelps of pain, as the pigeons helped themselves. Bracing for the assault, I hunched my shoulders and squeezed in beside Garth.

The photo I have shows an open-mouthed Daegan, arms out-stretched, the corn he'd just flung forever frozen in the air above him. Illanka, cute little blonde bombshell that she is, cringes in front of him with a pigeon perched on her head.

After a quick lunch at the Wimpy on the boardwalk, we spent the rest of the afternoon at the Aquarium and then headed back to Shaka's Rock for dinner. It was five o'clock when we arrived at the restaurant, a two-story building a couple of yards from the beach: "Best Seafood On The Coast."

Layne pulled into the parking lot and went through the drill of getting Margaret into the wheelchair before shoving it up a high, un-even sidewalk and the three steps leading to the restaurant door. We trooped in behind him and soon learned there was no lift to the sec-ond-story dining room. Now what? All this way, and no big night out for Garth and Margaret, who seldom left their dingy ninth-floor flat. I'd planned on splurging at the best restaurant we could find in the area. I wanted to make it a night to remember. The hostess, an attractive thir-ty-something, glanced around at our faces and then at the wheelchair. She pursed her lips thoughtfully.

"Agh, no, man, we must make a plan," she said, a look of determination building in her face. "Nordie! Baasie!" she cried in the direction of the bar.

In moments, two black African men dressed in gold-trimmed brown waiter uniforms appeared. In rapid-fire Afrikaans she asked them to carry Margaret's wheelchair up the stairs to the dining area. Layne, Irma, and I stared at each other and then burst out laughing.

"Margaret," Layne said, indicating the two men. "You up for this?"

She grinned. "Agh, why not?"

Garth smiled tentatively.

Jabbering to each other in some local African language, the two men positioned themselves, one in front, the other behind the wheelchair, and with a mighty "Hoomba!" they hefted Margaret into the air. Legs bowing with the strain, they battled their way up the narrow staircase. With the chair tipped almost perpendicular, Margaret strained forward, gripping the arms like someone on Disneyland's wildly twirling Mad Hatter's teacup ride.

"You all right, Margaret?" my brother kept calling after the swaying procession.

"I'm fine!" she called back.

They reached the top to a burst of applause from a big red-faced man in khaki shorts who looked like he'd stepped from a poster advertising Kruger National Park Game Reserve.

"Good work, boys!" he boomed, patting first one, then the other waiter on the shoulder. He turned to face the rest of us. "Welcome to my restaurant! Glad you made it," he added with a wink at Margaret. "This way, please."

We thanked the two men, Layne pressed a couple of coins into each of their hands, and we headed for our table with Garth pushing the wheelchair. Slipping my arm around his shoulders, I gave him a squeeze, then reached down and patted Margaret's hand.

"I'm all right," she said looking up at me with a shy smile.

With everyone seated, Margaret's wheelchair pushed up to the end of the table, and Garth to her right, menus were passed around.

"Now remember, order *anything* you like," I reminded everyone. "This is on me."

After much deliberation, joking, and changing of minds, Daegan ordered escargot, the girls, chicken, Layne, scampi, and Irma and I, lobster.

I glanced down the table at Garth and Margaret, who watched us with contented smiles. "Lobster, prawns, scampi?"

"Margaret can't have anything spicy," Garth said. "It upsets her tummy."

"Agh, yours too, man," Margaret said, nudging him.

"Well how about the lobster then?" I said. "That's not spicy. Please have whatever you want."

They glanced at each other then looked up at the waiter hovering expectantly beside them.

"Hamburgers please," they said almost in unison.

I sighed. I so wanted to splurge on them, give them a meal to remember.

"Hamburgers it is," the waiter said.

* * *

It was after eight o'clock when we returned to London House. Layne had dropped the rest of the family off at the condo before unloading Garth, Margaret, and me in front of the arcade. With plans to meet at the same spot in half an hour, Layne rode off to find parking. He was going to have to stay with the SUV; otherwise he'd risk losing it, or at least parts of it, to thieves. Against Garth's objections, I insisted on accompanying he and Margaret up to their flat.

To enter the lift, you had to pass through a floor-to-ceiling gate manned by a twenty-something black guy. Garth later told me this new arrangement had started shortly after apartheid ended. Behind him, another young guy, this one Indian, sat at a table with a white-ruled tablet where I was asked to write my name before being waved through. A couple of other guys hung around them, chatting.

"What happens if the lift isn't working?" I asked Garth as the lift lurched upward.

"We leave the wheelchair down there by the bloke's table and then I help Margaret up the stairs," he said.

She had at least sixty pounds on him. "You carry her?"

"No," he said with a grin, like I was having him on. "She puts her feet on the floor."

"These blokes will help sometimes," Margaret added.

After a creaking and groaning ride that threatened to conk out at any moment, we emerged on the fourth floor. The air was heavy with the stench of urine, feces, and something like lye with a hint of pine. My eyes watered.

"It's the public lavatories," Garth said noticing my expression. "They stink."

It struck me that we were on the fourth floor, not the ninth where they'd lived when I last visited. Garth opened the door to their flat and rolled Margaret in, flipping on the light switch as he passed.

Stepping inside, I gasped and clasped my hand over my mouth. A row of windows in the far wall were so grimy I doubted that the beam from a searchlight pressed against the glass could pass through. Two twin beds, one directly in front of a small TV, filled most of the room. The remaining space contained a tall dresser, mini fridge, and shelf piled with clothes. A couple of shirts and dresses were strung on a rod in an alcove. There was a small bathroom near the door.

"Garth," I gasped. "This is awful. I thought you lived on the ninth floor, I mean, from what I remember that room wasn't so . . . um, terrible."

He gave a nervous smile. "We had to move."

"I see that. Why didn't you tell me?"

He shrugged.

"Margaret?" I said.

"That's why Mac found the other place."

"Please tell me *exactly* what happened with that," I said.

From what I could gather, Garth had misunderstood the requirements of the Somerset. He'd put his name down in June as the manager had suggested, and given a thirty-day notice to London House. But when he showed up at the Somerset on the first of July, he was told that there was nothing available. He then had to scramble to find something immediately. London House accommodated him by moving them into this hellhole: one of their "spare" flats. And now they were waiting for a room to become available at the Somerset.

"Okay, so listen," I said brightly. "We're going to get you out of this place, all right?"

They both nodded.

"I must first give my notice," Garth said. He reached for a small, tattered notebook lying on the dresser and opened it. "I must give one month notice, otherwise I will lose my deposit."

I peered over his shoulder. Crude, uneven printing—all he'd managed to learn at the back of that special classroom at Frederick Knapp Primary School—filled a column on the left with numbers on the right: *flat, penshun, food, medsin*. His monthly obligations. There was a total at the bottom; a quick accounting told me it was accurate.

"Do you have enough money to live?" I said.

"Ja-a," he said, drawing out the word. Did I hear some doubt there?

"I'll put some money in your bank account," I said.

"I have money in there."

"Just in case you need more, all right?"

He shrugged. "All right."

"I get meals for pensioners," Margaret said.

"We sometimes share them at night," Garth said.

"Holy shit, they do that here?" I said.

"And then sometimes I stop and buy food down at the shop in the arcade or the one by the bus stop on my way home," Garth said. "I also stop and have a beer sometimes, too."

"You stop for a beer? In a bar?"

"Only one. Too many beers are not good for me."

I nodded, remembering how my Uncle Percy had given Garth a lecture about drinking after he got a call from the Coogee Beach manager when Garth still lived there, that he'd been observed in the lounge a couple of nights drinking more than was good for him. This was not long after our mother died. He stopped right away. Just like that.

"Well listen, I'd better—" I started, then stopped as I spotted a photograph partially hidden behind a stick of deodorant, fly spray, and a tin of black shoe polish on top of the dresser. Pasted onto a piece of cardboard, its top crudely trimmed, the photo was propped against the wall. I lifted it out.

There were three photos of me, all in sepia tones, two smaller ones pasted in the bottom and top left corners over an eight-by-six, a border with the printed words "Happy Days Studio, Mermaid Lido, Durban" barely visible in the bottom right corner. In the main photo I'm eleven years old, sitting atop slabs of waist-high rocks stacked around a flowerbed. A couple of scrawny plants peek out behind me. Below me is the boardwalk. To my right, rock steps lead up to Marine Parade. I'm smiling, my legs coyly arranged to one side, toes pointed, my wavy, chin-length, golden brown hair swept up to one side in a clip. I'm wearing a crisp, belted print dress. I can't tell the color, but it has a white overlapping collar, white cuffs around the almost elbow-length sleeves, and three rows of white zigzag trim near the knee-length hem. It's brand new—one of the "holiday" dresses my mother made. I could almost smell that new-dress odor: raw cotton, fresh and sunshiny, sewing machine oil, and a hint of tobacco from my mother's cigarettes. For the first

time in my life, I noticed the darts in the bodice, the flawless design, and remembered the times I stood there impatiently while she made adjustments so that it would turn out perfect.

I'd just sneaked out of our hotel room while my parents and three-year-old Garth took a nap. I was barefoot, as usual, but dolled up in my new dress this time, every pearl button tied, belt knotted just so. We'd arrived that morning. I caught hell later for sneaking out and allowing a strange man to

Me at Durban's Boardwalk

photograph me. I didn't tell my parents that the man kept trying to lift my dress a little higher to "show off my beautiful legs."

I turned to Garth. "I didn't know you had this."

"Ja," he said. "Mom had it in her box of things."

I thought they'd given me all the family photos when she, my dad, and Garth visited me in America not long before my dad died. I slid the photo back into place and glanced at my watch. Layne would be circling the block any minute.

"I've got to go, Layne's going to be worried," I said.

"Are we still going shopping?" Garth asked.

I'd forgotten we'd promised him a shopping spree. How could we do anything but find another place for them to live?

"Um," I began, and then stopped. I couldn't disappoint him. "Of course," I said. "We'll go shopping and then the two of you can spend tomorrow night with us. How does that sound?"

Beaming, he nodded. I hugged each of them as hard as I could.

Trying not to breathe in the fumes from the toilets, I ran down the stairs, only to be stopped at the bottom by the young elevator operator.

"Please, you must sign out," he said, holding out the pen.

I scribbled my initials and bounced in place while he opened the gate. I hurried down the arcade. With each step, a wretchedness settled deep into my bones. Finding Layne double-parked, I slumped into the SUV. As he swung back into traffic, I told him what I had seen.

"Hey, Mom, this is fixable," he said, shooting anxious glances at me while he drove. "Okay?"

I nodded but couldn't stop the tears trickling down my cheeks. And at some point during the journey back to the condo, I got it into my head that I was imposing on Layne and his family—that I should be the one, the only one, taking care of my brother's problems. He was my responsibility.

My wretched attitude, along with my conviction that I alone was responsible for Garth, had the collective effect of making the entire family act like they'd somehow offended me. They spoke in hushed tones around me. Locked in my vault of doom, I couldn't set them straight. My forthrightness had abandoned me. I wanted to curl up and die.

Fifteen

THE FOLLOWING MORNING, with tear-swollen eyelids and that pinched lift to my top lip I get after a crying jag, I accompanied Irma and the kids to the beach while Layne checked on the Somerset. Despite my protestations that I should accompany him, he insisted on going alone.

"You'll just be in the way," he joked, then quickly checked to see if I was offended.

"Oh, go ahead and hurt my feelings," I said and managed a grin.

He returned at noon after storming out of the Somerset in frustration. Turns out they did let to the handicapped at a nominal rate, but it was rare that they had an opening. As far as Layne could tell, management had led Garth on. Yes, yes, write your name down if you like. Silly retarded fellow.

On the way back to the condo, Layne picked up a listing of flats in the area, then spent an hour telephoning around and driving to a number of places. He narrowed it down to a couple of prospects: a residential hotel and the Albany Hotel. It was unlikely we would find a sweet deal like the one offered at the Somerset. Layne offered to help me subsidize Garth and Margaret's meager wages, then suggested we check on the accommodations the following day; we were due to pick up Garth and Margaret to take them shopping.

Layne and I found Garth standing alone on the sidewalk outside London House. I shuddered at the sight of the place and pasted a smile on my face.

"Where's Margaret?" I asked as Garth climbed into the SUV.

"The lift is broken," he said.

My melancholy deepened. "We'll buy her something," I said. "What does she need?"

"Maybe a nightie," Garth said. "She'll need one for the winter."

"What size?"

"Very big."

Layne found a shopping mall that included gambling a couple of miles north of Marine Parade. Apparently the Calvinistic Dutch Reformed Church had lost its grip. Layne drove into the underground parking structure and pulled into a parking space with a one-handed twirl of the SUV's steering wheel, grinning back at Garth as he did. Garth rewarded him with a broad smile and a giggle, his dentures a blazing strip of white in the semi-darkness. My heart constricted. My little brother was an old man.

With Layne leading the way, we all headed toward the mall entrance. I didn't see the concrete stanchion and rammed it with my bare, sandaled toes.

"Damn!"

"You okay, Mom?"

"Who put that bloody thing there?" I hobbled around in a circle to shake off the pain.

"The workers put them there for the motorcars so they don't run into the wall," Garth said in his slow and careful way. He dropped to one knee and rubbed my toes. "You must be more careful, San."

I started to protest—he was getting his pants dirty on the filthy floor, I was being a big baby—but then I felt the strength of his fingers and stopped. I looked down at his hunched back, the daring red suspenders attached to faded blue jeans, the matching denim shirt he'd bargained for in the Indian market three miles from his flat, the grey socks, the worn-out work shoes—twenty-five years on the job—and the address book sticking out of his back pocket.

It was like I was seeing him for the first time. He was his own person. Despite his limitations, he'd been taking care of business for a while now. Not only for himself but for Margaret as well. Perhaps our parents' death had been the making of the man. My heart swelled with pride and love: clean, free, unencumbered emotions I don't ever remember feeling for him. Had I always been too quick to take blame for things that weren't my fault because I'd never known where to draw the line? Had my distorted sense of responsibility been the underpinning of all my relationships? I touched the back of his head.

"I'm all right now, thanks. You're getting dirty."

He rose to his feet and brushed his pants. "Yes. This floor is a bloody mess."

"D'you think you can walk?" Layne asked, grinning. "Or should I carry you?"

"Funny man," I said.

Garth grinned at Layne. "Funny man."

We headed for the mall, Garth's hand in the small of my back to guide me. For the rest of the trip, he kept telling me when a step was coming up. Before we arrived at the escalator he warned me that I would have to hold on to the railing.

I ended up buying Garth jeans, shirts, pajamas, socks, shoes, and towels. It surprised me that he knew exactly what he wanted and wasn't afraid to say so. More than I can say for myself most of the time. I couldn't find a nightie for Margaret, so I vowed to send her one when I got home, where it was still winter.

Later that night, Garth, in his new pajamas, sat on the couch staring wide-eyed at the antics of Bianca and Illanka as they shyly lip-synched into a small table lamp to a song by Avril Lavigne, Daegan playing air guitar. Layne, Irma, and I sat on the verandah and talked. I told them what I'd been feeling.

"You had us worried," Irma said.

"I've never known you to be at a loss for words before," Layne said.

"Maybe that's a good thing," I said, remembering how I'd always filled in answers for Larry. But maybe things were changing.

"Oh, and don't ever pull that bullshit that you're being an imposition again," Layne said. "I'm your family too, you know."

"All right, all right," I said, grinning sheepishly. "I can have a freak out, can't I?"

"Just one," Layne said.

The following morning, a Sunday, we drove Garth back to London House. I'd hoped we could spend the day together, but he insisted on returning to the flat to take care of Margaret. She needed her bath, he said.

* * *

On a whim, I looked up the address of the Coogee Beach Hotel. It was mid-afternoon when we pulled up in front of the place. I checked the address. This dull red building with barred windows and a metal grill–covered front door wasn't the Coogee I remembered. Where was the wide front entrance? The brass door handles? The cheery yellow paint? The woman who answered the door confirmed that this was indeed the Coogee Beach Hotel, but it was now a retirement home. Garth didn't qualify, he was too young. Besides, there was a waiting list. We asked if she knew of any other accommodations nearby. She didn't, but offered to get the local listings of available flats. How about a nice cup of tea? she asked.

We sat on the verandah in comfortable if shabby cane chairs, sipped cups of South Africa's famous Rooibos tea, and talked about the old Coogee and all the changes that had taken place in post-apartheid South Africa. The smell of cabbage wafted from inside the building; muted voices leaked from the second floor. I glanced around for something familiar that would remind me of the last time I saw my mother, but there was nothing. My thoughts strayed and I thought about my dad and the last time I saw him.

It was seven years after I left Africa when the whole family came over to the States to visit us. He'd received the "golden handshake" from the black Zambian government after the country gained independence from Britain. This was a payout to white mine workers to get rid of them so that the jobs could be given to black Africans. Unfortunately, they were unskilled. Combined with plummeting copper prices, the government drove the mining industry into an almost fatal dive. My father got a job down at Kimberley diamond mines, where he intended to keep working "until he keeled over," as he put it. He didn't last two years.

But at least he got the money he needed to set up my mom and brother if he should die before they did. No one expected him to go first, not with all my mother's health issues. An old school friend, just recently back in my life, recalls these ailments as the "vapors." I thought I was the only one who thought of her illnesses this way.

My mother got the call from Kimberley Hospital at one o'clock that fateful morning. My dad had stumbled into Emergency gasping and complaining of chest pains, thrown up, and died minutes later on the gurney as they wheeled him into surgery. She hadn't heard him leave the house. He'd driven the twenty miles to the hospital on his own. The only other time he'd been sick was when he was hospitalized for five days after being gassed underground in Nkana's main shaft, where he operated the double-decker "cages" up and down the two-mile-deep shaft.

The evening following his death, I got the news from a Western Union employee over the phone in a supervisor's office at AMF Voit, a sporting goods manufacturer in Costa Mesa where I worked the graveyard shift as a word processor. I'd been in the States for nine years by then and hated my job. I stood there holding the phone long after the operator hung up, ricocheting wildly between disbelief and terror. It had to be a mistake. Sixty-five was too young to die. It was only after I walked out to tell the supervisor that the tears poured out.

I spent the next six months going through the motions for Darin and Layne and John, but I kept thinking of ways to die. Was that overpass high enough? How many aspirin did it take? I just couldn't wake to another morning knowing he was gone: the one person in my life who truly knew me, who told me that no matter what, I could always come home. I kept telling people he wasn't supposed to die; he'd promised he wouldn't. Crazy talk, but for once I didn't care what people thought. John was the most supportive he'd ever been.

Being the pragmatic people we South Africans are, I didn't fly home right away. Money was tight. John and I had just purchased a house, and the hefty mortgage hung over us. "Pay cash or don't buy it" was how we'd been raised. Besides, as my mother told me over the phone two days later when I finally reached her in Kimberley, there was no need to come all the way home. Dad was gone, and his ashes had already been scattered. She spoke about him with unfamiliar tenderness.

And now as I sat there on the old Coogee's verandah, I struggled to remember the last time I saw my mother. It had been at the Coogee, shortly after dad died. It was September, the beginning of the hot season. I'd finally made the journey back to South Africa with Layne and Darin. A year later I would leave John. She would've been wearing a sleeveless dress—purchased now, not sewn on her Singer machine the way both our clothes were when I was growing up. Her thick, shoulder-length, greying hair would have been pulled back behind her ears with a matching ribbon. She would've been wearing sandals, a holdover from all those years of living in the bush. And she would've been smoking. I rarely saw her, or my father for that matter, without a cigarette. He handled one like Ernest Hemingway, cigarette stuck all the way into the crook of his middle and forefinger, while she sometimes used an ivory cigarette holder. Even though I've always hated cigarettes, I must admit that she smoked more elegantly than anyone I've ever seen.

So there we were in the Coogee Beach Hotel: me, my mom, Garth, Darin, and Layne. We sat around one of those knee-high, heavy cocktail tables in the lounge, like so many of the lounges I'd visited with my parents over the years as a child: Rhokana Mine Club for "sundowners"— 5 p.m. cocktails of gin and tonic for my mother, brandy and coke for my dad—or, when we traveled down to South Africa, The Victoria Falls Hotel or The Lion and Monkey near Bulawayo in Zimbabwe. Then there was that three-month trip up to Malawi, Tanzania, and Kenya through the Tsavo National Park, Ngorogoro Crater, and every other game reserve my father could find along the way, on the map or not. We stayed in bush hotels and had sundowners in lounges manned by red fez–wearing waiters in white uniforms.

The four of us sat in front of the elevator. Darin and Layne got into one of their endless shoving matches while Garth sat in a chair beside my mother, grinning at their antics. My mom and I drank tea with milk and two sugars—just like Leffy used to prepare in our Nkana mine house—bringing the cups, nestled in their saucers, up to our chins before sipping. She was pleasant, leaning forward every so often to flick ash into one of the hotel's many ashtrays, legs elegantly crossed, her face unreadable. Did she hug the boys when we arrived? Did we hug? Surely we did. The meeting flits in and out of my memory like a hummingbird.

We all walked the two blocks down to the beach and stopped at the wall below Marine Parade. Mom and I leaned our elbows on the wall and stared out at the sea. Darin and Layne charged down to the beach and stuffed sand down each other's pants. Garth stood upright beside my mother, a familiar expectant, bewildered expression on his face.

"It was hard throwing away your dad's mess," she said without looking at me. Dad's "mess" was a drawer filled with pencil stubs, scraps of scribbled notes, monthly bills, random lengths of wire, nuts and bolts, and various small tools, along with nests of cigarette ash, those long columns that would build at the end of his neglected cigarettes and then fall into the drawer whenever he took a drag.

I nodded, feeling a fresh pang of loss.

"Uncle Percy helped us move," she said. "The Coogee is a decent enough place, hm?"

"Well, at least you're close to the sea."

"I don't like the beach."

"I know."

"All that sand."

"I would give anything to have had just one more moment with Dad before he died," I blurted, my eyes filling with tears. I couldn't look at her.

"It was quick," she said softly. "That's what they told me, anyway." From the corner of my eye, I saw her bow her head.

I don't remember who broke the silence that followed; I just remember her flicking her spent cigarette onto the beach, and the prickle of annoyance that kind of behavior always evoked in me. My last contact with my mother was a shoulders-only hug on the sidewalk outside the hotel.

The memory flooded me with guilt and agitation. I popped to my feet. Layne shot me an uneasy glance and continued to chat with the woman from the Coogee. I muttered something about stretching my legs and wandered over to one of the barred windows to peer inside. All I could see of the formerly sun-filled foyer of the old Coogee were dim shapes. And then I noticed the brass gleam of the elevator. My breath caught in my throat. The elevator. That's where she died of a heart attack. I found out about it three months later. A telegram from Uncle Percy, misdelivered to an empty house across the street from the subterranean, jury-rigged room Larry and I were renting in Laguna Beach from that young couple who sold pot.

The new tenant delivered the telegram as I pulled into the driveway from work in my VW GTI—the first car I bought in my new life as a single American citizen. Thanking the man for going to the trouble, I took the crumpled, brittle envelope from him, thinking how brilliant these Americans were with their advertisements, a fakey missive from some rich and textured past to draw me in to buy something. It took a while for the message to sink in.

"Anne passed away. Stop. Heart attack. Stop. Sorry. Stop. Percy."

I stared down at the words, panic mounting. My thoughts fuzzed out. I wondered if she'd received my Mother's Day card. Had I sent it in time? I checked the date of the telegram. February. She'd been dead for three months. I could hardly wait for Larry to get home. We'd been married for two months by then. I was ashamed that I couldn't cry.

I called Uncle Percy. He'd been "surprised" I hadn't responded earlier. Earlier? Three months earlier? What the hell? Why hadn't he called? Tried harder to get hold of me? Had he known all along what a heartless daughter I'd been?

Now, as I stood staring at the elevator through the Coogee's window, I wondered what it was between us. Why we never had a single conversation that didn't make me feel in the wrong, uncomfortable, or irritated at her. Even after I had Darin, those fourteen hours of labor, I didn't look to her for comfort. Other than being at the hospital the entire time during my labor and birth—albeit in the waiting room, as was the custom in those days—I don't remember her being around much during my first terrifying months of motherhood. And she lived not more than a couple of miles away in Nkana.

Soon after I started menstruating at thirteen, I overheard her confiding to a friend that she'd told me all about the birds and the bees. She actually used those words, the birds and the bees. Well, she hadn't. When I finally managed to confess that I'd found blood on my panties—I wasn't completely ignorant of what it might mean, although I also had an obsessive fear that every little change in my health meant bilharzia, a disease caused by swimming in the Kafue river that made your pee turn black and killed you after a while, something my mother was always warning me against—she got this sappy, knowing expression on her face, rose to her feet, and returned with a giant sanitary pad and garter-like straps. Face blazing, I listened as she explained how it worked. "Do you want me to help you?" she asked. I would've died first.

Over the years, I convinced myself that the strain between us was primarily my fault. Me and my headstrong ways and cheeky mouth. Always getting in the last word, impatient with the way she continued to explain something long after I'd gotten it, how she kept talking through her sobs after she'd been drinking. How she never let me forget my transgressions. Truth was, I wished I had someone else for a mother, someone who wasn't stingy with praise, someone who wasn't always finding fault, someone who had my back. She'd believed those sanctimonious neighbors she loathed when we lived in Welkom when they told her they saw me smoking behind the OK Bazaars, when she knew how much I despised the habit. And when I'd broken down in tears begging her to believe me, she'd wanted to know why I was becoming so hysterical if I was innocent. She'd stood with my grandfather against me. Later, when we'd returned to Nkana, she'd pulled my new girlfriend aside—I was eleven and new in town—and told her to watch out, I would lead her astray. A badge of coolness later, but at the time this warning mortified me; I just wanted to fit in.

And then there she was barefoot and parading around in her slip in front of my girlfriends and a prospective boyfriend when I was fifteen. What was that about? Craving attention? I finally decided that's what her "vapors" had been all about, those repetitive episodes of obscure medical conditions with long names that brought various mine doctors to the house. All those illnesses that had her laid up, that had my dad waiting on her. I also realized that I probably got more of my father's attention than she did.

"Oh, Mom," I whispered.

If I'd been left to my father's permissive ways, who knows how I would've turned out: Coca-Cola and potato chips for breakfast, pudding for dinner, all the sweets I wanted to eat; allowed to wear whatever I wanted, allowed to get out of homework, allowed to go to bed whenever I wanted. Instead, she tried to shape me, tried to corral my "wild" streak even as my father encouraged it. And then there were all those socks and jerseys, dresses, shorts, and blouses she knitted and sewed. The Robin Hood costume, complete with felt hat and green leggings, that she made the year I turned five; I even had a bow, a quiver of arrows, and a cow's horn strung around my neck. I won first prize in the Mine Club fancy dress competition.

All my ballet dresses, my Harlequin costume in the school play at St. John's Convent School when I was fourteen. The best costume they'd ever seen. That's how she showed her love for me. And what of her essential shyness? And the anguish of dealing with my father's infidelities? And Garth. Oh, the disappointment and suffering his afflictions caused her.

My Robin Hood Costume

Tears slipped down my cheeks.

"Mom?" Layne said.

I wiped my tears with my sleeve. "Hm?"

"Ready to go?"

"That I am."

I linked my arm in his and hugged his side. We headed down the walkway.

"So what was that all about?" Layne asked, holding the car door open for me.

"Oh, I was just thinking about my mom," I said, sliding into the car. I'd tell him later that the grandmother he met once died not far from where we sat.

"Is that good or bad?"

"Not bad."

He considered me for a moment then closed the door behind me. We headed for the Albany. To my relief, the place was a lot like the old Coogee but with a security guard. We filled out an application and returned to "Mellyboo." I called Garth and told him what was going on.

The following morning, Layne returned to the Albany and was told that Garth and Margaret could move into a second-floor room, complete with TV and maid service, on the first of February, five weeks away. Layne was assured that the lift was reliable. He co-signed. Now all I had to do was make sure I came up with the needed money to subsidize Garth and Margaret.

That night Layne and I made the trip back to "Hades" and told Garth and Margaret the good news. Broad grins lit their faces. I told Garth he had to give his notice as soon as possible. His grin melted and he literally wrung his hands. I assured him that no matter what happened with the deal at the Albany, he would not be forced back into another hell like he'd just been through. Not if Layne and I had anything to do with it. Garth shifted from foot to foot and looked doubtful.

"Layne will come down from Centurion and move you into the Albany. You can go and check out the place, if you like," I said.

"What's the address?" he asked, and reached for his address book in his back pocket.

Layne told him. Garth wrote slowly and laboriously, snapped the book shut, stuck it back in his pocket, and reached for his other notebook on the dresser. He continued writing. "I can only give them notice on the first of January," he said.

"Of course," I said. My little brother, the stickler. So like our mother, so like me.

We left for Centurion the following morning.

Sixteen

IT WAS A true South African Christmas Day spent at Irma's sister's house in Ellisras, a coal mining town three hundred miles from Centurion, in the heart of the bushveld. Along with a fake miniature baobab tree decorated with tiny colored glass balls and wisps of silver tinsel, there was the customary oil drum that had been cut in half lengthwise to serve as a braaivleis grill. Beneath a blazing sun, kids splashed in and out of the pool, climbed a tree tall as Jack's beanstalk, and teased Shorty, a fox terrier.

The customary braaivleis social scene used to irritate me to no end—the women sitting on kitchen chairs on the lawn in a circle or in the kitchen while the men stood in a clump around the braaivleis drum, talking rugby and drinking beer for what seemed hours on end—but now it seemed solid and endearing.

I closed my eyes, the sun warm and comforting, and listened to the Afrikaans conversation between Irma's family, congratulating myself on how much I remembered from my almost three years of compulsory Afrikaans classes in Rustenburg, Welkom, and Barberton. My daughter-in-law had also continued to send me Afrikaans jokes or some little saying in emails to keep me limber. From what sounded like miles away, Irma's mother called my name. I'd drifted off. I jerked awake to see her kneeling in front of a quilt spread out on the grass behind me. Patting it, she told me in Afrikaans to come have a little lie-down. There was something so intimate and caring about this I wanted to hug her. I thanked her, lay on my back on the quilt, and, shielding my eyes, stared up at the sky. These were good people who meant what they said, whose word you could count on, and to whom family meant everything, at any cost. I hadn't even realized that this was something I'd had growing up, that I'd taken for granted. I curled up in a ball and slept as long as I liked.

On the journey home at twilight, the horizon turned lava red and a storm suddenly appeared out of nowhere, turning the clouds an apocalyptic black with eerie silver edges. Layne pulled over and I snapped photos until nightfall ruined it all. I was reminded once again why I loved Africa: the way it pulsed with life, raw, exuberant, astonishing, unpredictable, and how much it was a part of me. Back in the car, Larry came up again in conversation, as he had throughout my visit—had he taken any surf trips lately, had he finally started making pots again, would I ever be able to persuade him to return to South Africa for a visit? I could answer the first one truthfully, with a little secret irony thrown in—lots of trips to Mexico. The last one I hedged on: "You know Larry and traveling." It was uncomfortable. I felt like a liar. But I just couldn't bring myself to tell them the truth.

On New Year's Eve we made tacos from scratch with ingredients I'd brought from the States. We all helped and Layne made margaritas. I sat by the pool sipping my second margarita while everyone else cleaned up. Tomorrow a whole new year would begin. Larry and I used to make our New Year's resolutions together, which usually included finding new ways to express our artistic creativity, making more visits to museums and art shows, and taking more trips, as well as finishing projects around the house. One of my recurring resolutions was to slow down and take naps; his always included "more nookie." The resolutions stopped after the affair. What was going to happen to us? Would he even bother to call tomorrow? At that moment, both Layne and Irma hugged me from behind. I burst out crying.

"Hey, what's this?" Layne asked, sinking into a chair next to me. Irma charged into the house for a box of tissues.

"Garth's fine," Layne continued. "It's all sorted."

Irma returned and handed me a tissue.

"So what's wrong?" Layne said.

I blew my nose and waved him off.

"No," Layne said. "Talk to me."

Hesitantly at first, I told them about what I'd been going through with Larry, including his affair. Not all the sordid details, but enough, which felt like way too much anyway.

"God, this feels really weird . . . talking to my kid about this."

"Man!" Layne said. "I can't believe he'd do something like that. I would never have taken him for a Don Juan."

"According to him there was no actual 'affair.' She made 'the move'—grateful, apparently, that he'd been so kind and supportive during her battle to leave an abusive husband. That much I gathered—without much help from him, let me tell you. But of course, I don't know anything for sure. He would never discuss it, told me it was too painful, said he couldn't bear to hurt me any more. Which, of course, made me imagine all kinds of things."

"Why didn't you tell me all this before?" Layne asked.

"Oh, yeah, like I was going to tell you something like this? It's embarrassing, to say the least. Not only that, I'd hoped the two of us could work through everything."

"Maybe he's having a mid-life crisis," Layne said. "And now he's on a . . . walkabout."

"Walkabout. I like that. Sounds like he's looking for answers and will eventually come home enlightened and committed, ready to make changes. Only thing is, he's already had a mid-life crisis—maybe even a couple. All I know is that he has zero interest in working on our relationship."

"What's his family think about all this?" Irma said.

"Actually, I don't know what they think. They don't know details, but they do know about the affair. I finally told his eldest sister in desperation one day, years after it happened, because he, of course, wasn't talking, and I just couldn't get over it. I think I told her because I hoped that as family she had some particular insight, something I didn't know about him that would help me. Her advice? Men will be men, and that he was more open with me than he'd ever been with anyone else, including his own family. That's not saying much. Anyway, I asked her not to tell the rest of the family. That didn't happen. A couple of Thanksgivings later, they were all making sly and very funny innuendos about him and the affair. Like, hadn't they seen this little surfer kid down at the beach with bow legs who looked just like Larry? Come to think of it, why did I think it was funny? Pretty sick, actually. Maybe because I was glad somebody was talking about it, even though it was underhanded. His reaction was a blank look, like they were talking about somebody else. He didn't say a word."

"And what about now, with him taking off for weeks on end?" Layne said. "Are they there for you?"

"Oh, a couple of phone calls in the beginning, asking if he was back. No words of concern for me. No visits, not unless he was around. Someone in the family, I can't remember who, said that he asked them to stay away. He said he didn't. I believe him. He doesn't give enough of a shit to lie about it. I just think the whole family hates conflict. Oh, and one more thing—someone let drop a remark at one of the family weddings I missed that if I hadn't been holed up in my studio writing, he wouldn't have taken off. They were probably only 'playing,' right? Everything's a joke. But it hurt. And it pissed me off. So fucking unfair. When I told him, he thought it was the funniest thing he'd ever heard, said something like, 'Well, you should've paid more attention to me, right?'" I trailed off, drained. I rose to my feet. "Okay, my loves. Enough. I'm taking my sorry drunken ass to bed."

"Well, one good thing about all of this," Layne said, draping his arm over my shoulders. "Now, you'll have to come home and live with us."

"What about Sweetpea and Jake?"

"Oh, they can come too. He blew it."

"Thanks, hon, but you know how I feel about Africa."

"We'll work on her," Irma said to Layne.

I grinned at her then turned to go. "Okay, loveyoubye."

"Loveyoubye," they repeated in unison.

I could feel their eyes on me as I climbed the staircase to the bedroom Illanka had given up for my stay. I fell into the queen-size bed, determined not to dwell on Larry and our problems. I was asleep in moments, caressed by a cool evening breeze that blew in through the half-open windows, making the sheer white curtains billow into the room like sails.

I awoke in a panic and I glanced at the clock: 1:00 a.m. I'd only been asleep for a couple of hours. Did something bad happen last night? Suddenly I was recalling every word of my conversation with Irma and Layne. Why did everything seem so calamitous in the middle of the night? I groaned. What a blabbermouth idiot I'd been.

What must they think of me? What must they think of Larry? He still hadn't called. Was he okay? Maybe something had happened to him. Who was taking take care of Sweetpea and Jake? What the hell was I doing with my life? Why hadn't I let him move out like he'd wanted to when I realized he'd had the affair? Why couldn't I get it through my head that he would never be capable of facing the conflict his betrayal had created? Hadn't he told me himself that it was too painful to face? And how could I have hoped that his comment, "I'm here, aren't I?" was a concession to working on our marriage? The playlist in my mind, constructed over twenty-five years of trying to make sense of his actions and the affair droned on and on, accompanied by my habitual thoughts that I just hadn't found the right words to reach him.

My pajamas damp with sweat, I leapt out of bed and opened the windows as far as they would go, then stood in front of them breathing in the cool, frangipani-scented night air. A dog—or was that a jackal?—trotted down the street below me, setting off motion detector lights. Couldn't be a jackal, too much civilization. In the distance, the lights of Pretoria—or was that Johannesburg? What direction was I facing? God, how could the horizon be lit up so brightly in South Africa? So much change. Change I'd never dreamed possible. *I* had to make a change. I had to move on.

I had to get some sleep.

I lay back down on the bed and wished Sweetpea and Jake were there so I could curl up with them. I tried to quiet my mind, but it was too late. I was too keyed up. The hours ticked by as I thrashed around the bed and did battle with every thought that popped up. On and on it went, until I felt like I'd gone over some kind of edge where nothing made sense.

Finally at 5 a.m., exhausted and light-headed, I dragged myself up, sat on the edge of the bed, and turned on the lamp. If I could just write down a couple of rational thoughts, ideas, anything, I'd be able to find my way back to sanity. I reached for my journal, rested it on the side table, and picked up my pen with shaking hands. All I managed to write was one word—"I"—over and over again, the pen slippery in my hands from sweat. Feeling desperate, I flipped over to a new page. Please. Some other word. Anything. My mind was as blank as the page. I slammed down my journal and the pen, which bounced and flipped onto the floor.

Clutching myself, I rocked back and forth. Is this what happens when a person goes mad? And what exactly does that mean? I stopped. God, what kind of self-indulgence was this? I bent down, snatched up my pen and wrote out the word "CAT" in capital letters. I stared down at the word and started to cry, suddenly my seven-year-old self again. On that day, all those years ago, I'd awoken in the middle of the afternoon with a raging fever and charged into my mother's bedroom in a panic, unable to spell the word "cat." She had been furious at me for waking her from a nap and wouldn't spell the word for me. This time I got the word down in big bold letters.

Wiping my tears on my pajama sleeve, I took a deep breath. Okay, I told myself, no thinking, no being clever, no worrying about spelling or the outcome, the words could be ugly and misshapen and the bottom of the Ys could just be little sticks instead of my usual expansive loops. I didn't have to know what I was going to write, it didn't have to make sense, it didn't have to be tidy. And then I forced myself to wing it. The words that came to mind almost died in the making; they seemed made up, trite, they were words I wanted to rip apart as soon as they were formed.

This is what I wrote: "I deserve to be happy. It's not only up to me to save my marriage. I have to make a choice. It's Him or Me. From this day forward, in every situation, especially where Larry is concerned, my mantra will be the following: 'Is this making me happy? Is this moving me forward?'" I lifted my pen and stared down at what I'd written. What simplistic crap. How were these stupid words going to get me unstuck? But something had shifted deep inside me. I stared out the window. The pale gold and rose vapors of dawn had crept above the horizon, replacing the stark glare of electric lights of the night before. I let go, lay back down, and slept until 10 a.m.

A week later, the entire family drove me back to Oliver Tambo airport. My flight was due to leave at 10:30 p.m. They snaked through the line with me and then ran alongside the barrier after I'd gone through security, cupping their hands to their mouths and calling out that it wasn't too late to turn around.

The journey onto the aircraft was a lonely one. I plopped into my seat and stared out the airplane window until all I could see of Johannesburg were pinpricks of light. Four hundred miles to the east, on the coast, Garth would be asleep, ready to start a new phase in his life. He was the one with mental disabilities, and yet he'd managed his life a whole lot better than I had. In twenty-four hours I'd be back in the States with another chance to manage my own life.

I thought back to my resolution. In all things involving Larry, it would be, in capital letters: "IS THIS MAKING ME HAPPY? IS THIS MOVING ME FORWARD?" That had been one helluva night. I'd stood at the crossroads. I'd made a decision.

Seventeen

MY TWENTY-TWO-hour flight back to Los Angeles from Johannesburg was fifteen minutes late. All around me, passengers were on their cell phones. Mine stayed in my pocket. Larry didn't do cell phones. It would mean being available. Besides, his hearing was going. As usual I would just head for what would turn out to be the wrong exit, and he would circle the airport looking for me. Maybe for hours. A comedy of errors. And then he'd get pissed. Fuck him. I retrieved my rollaway and strode up the ramp, taking big, liberating steps.

Clumps of people crowded the entrance, some craning their necks toward the horde streaming out around me. Couples and families came together with hugs and joyful cries. No one here to meet me. Not that he usually came all the way into the airport to meet my plane.

Ignoring the People Mover, I strode toward Baggage Claim. The sun broke through the mass of rainclouds that just half an hour ago had spread out below the plane like grey cotton wool and streamed through the two-story-high windows of the terminal. The world outside was new again, washed clean.

My red suitcase was one of the last to come snoozing around the baggage carousel. Instead of being agitated by the delay—no reason to hurry—I waited until it reappeared and then bent over to grab it. An arm reached around me, brushing my waist, and swept my suitcase from the carousel. I turned. My heart quickened.

"You came to meet me!"

He was dressed in a dark grey Surfrider sweatshirt, dark blue knee-length board shorts, and "dress" flip-flops. His long, fly-away grey hair framed his face in its usual mess of half-combed tangles.

"How was the trip?" he asked, as if he always came to help me retrieve my bags, as if I hadn't been gone for three weeks—as if we were an old happily married couple.

"How come you came all the way into the airport?"

"Oh, why? I shouldn't have?"

"You don't usually. In fact, I'm trying to remember if you ever did."

"Sure I have," he said with a crooked grin. "Haven't I? Anyway, I was early. Do you mind?"

So nonchalant, so disarming. A clap of thunder shook the building as I fell in step beside him. And then he was asking in his warm, hypnotic voice about my brother. This from the man who hadn't bothered to call me once in South Africa, not to wish me Merry Christmas or Happy New Year, or even to see if I had made it safely. And instead of becoming defensive when I chastised him for not calling me, he seemed mildly surprised that I expected him to.

It struck me how pale, even ghostly, his eyes appeared. There was no life in them. A fist wrapped itself around my heart. Depression, or whatever was eating at him, was taking its toll.

As we made our way to the car in the underground parking lot and headed for the freeway, he told me how Sweetpea had made him pay for my abandoning her—she didn't eat for two days and wouldn't leave her donut bed—the crappy surfing conditions of late, and how he'd spent Christmas and New Year's Eve alone (which was the way he liked it). Other than that, there was nothing new.

It started to sprinkle as we swung onto the freeway. He asked about my visit. Determined not to get sucked back into the ease of his company and twenty-five years of habit, I told him I'd had a good time, without going into detail. I had to keep my wits about me. I had to remember to keep asking myself those questions that had been wrenched from the depths of my being that soul-searching night in South Africa. In all things involving Larry, it would be, in capital letters: IS THIS MAKING ME HAPPY? IS THIS MOVING ME FORWARD?

Every now and again he asked another question about Layne, Garth, South Africa, or Irma and the kids. I gave him short answers and stared out the window. Fifteen minutes later he asked another question, like he was making polite conversation. The steady slap of the windshield wipers was deafening in the silences. But then when he brought up my brother again, I found myself unable to curtail my enthusiasm, and before long I was rattling on about everything that had happened, including my epiphany with Garth. Keeping his eyes on the road, he nodded now and then.

Soon we were reminiscing about Layne and when they added the loft and dining room to our house fifteen years earlier—all the beer they drank, the miscalculations they made, and the day Larry, standing on a ladder and working on a lattice for the front fence, almost cut his penis off with the Skilsaw, how he held his ravaged member wrapped in a kitchen towel and sent Layne charging around looking for a completely inappropriate butterfly Band-Aid before Layne drove him to the emergency room, where he got twelve stitches. We laughed.

Larry took a detour to buy me a cappuccino at my favorite coffee place in Newport Beach. The clouds broke and the sun burst through in time to melt over the horizon in a blaze of crimson and gold as we turned onto Pacific Coast Highway and headed south toward Laguna Beach.

When we got home, he made me wait outside the gate while he went in to get the dogs. He flung open the gate and then stood to one side while they charged out, Jake pogoing up and down beside me like a wind-up toy as Sweetpea launched herself at me. I dropped to my knees and hugged and kissed them both while Larry took my suitcase into the house and got us a beer to celebrate my return home. Later, he went out for pizza and we sat eating on the couch, watching basketball with Sweetpea and Jake between us. It wasn't ten minutes until he handed me the remote.

"Watch whatever you want."

I thought back to the times he'd called himself "doggy boy," for giving up the remote whenever I wanted to watch something he didn't. He loved this term and used it in lots of situations. It was his way of letting me know he didn't like being told what to do and that I was "bullying" him. I didn't watch much TV, so I would end up getting pissed, flinging down the remote, and heading for bed. He'd get his way and I'd feel like a jerk. I took the remote and flipped through the channels for ten minutes before I found myself drifting off.

"Okay, that's it, I'm exhausted, time for bed," I said and stood. Resisting the urge to give him a goodnight peck, I headed toward the stairs with Sweetpea and Jake on my heels.

"Turncoats," he called after us.

I spent the next week catching up at work, getting back into my exercise routine, and engaging in the little bit of cleaning that I do every time I return from a holiday. Larry had been busy working on the house while I was gone, adding those parts of the roof fascia he'd never gotten around to finishing and filling in the bottom part of the outside walls with river rock. He told me to think about what colors to paint the outside of the house. All the things I'd nagged him to do for years. Something had changed. I shelved the ultimatum I'd set before I left: counseling or divorce. This was making me happy. This seemed to be moving me forward.

He'd also been reorganizing the garage: his surfboards were neatly lined up in the rafters, the clutter of tools, spray cans, and Chevy Nomad parts on top of the cabinets had been stashed away, and four boxes of his T-shirts were stacked in one corner. These were part of his thirty-year-old collection of shirts that had all but taken over our one closet at one point, some of them threadbare and stained, some still with price tags on them. A couple of years earlier I'd told him, trash or garage. All that remained in the house now were the twenty or so he'd chosen for day-to-day wear—his intention was to rotate them over time with the stored ones. Along with these boxes of T-shirts were empty Sierra Nevada and Pacifico beer boxes filled with odds and ends. He'd also done a lot of work on the Nomad.

I was glad to see him engrossed like this. Even so, I held back, reminding myself that nothing had permanently changed between us. Sometimes, though, I couldn't control my exuberant self from bubbling up. He was trying to work through whatever dissatisfaction had driven him to Mexico. He'd once told me that I shouldn't take his "crap" personally. This was before the affair, when he'd given me an article on "Male Menopause" to read.

So I bumped along, holding back from snuggling up to him, from kissing those same tantalizing patches of perfectly curling dark hair on his wrists that had me jumping half-naked into the Jacuzzi with him on our first date. One thing at a time. When I couldn't resist hugging him, he'd respond by giving me an embrace, along with a pat on the back: Okay, we're done now. This from the man who not so long ago had taken any sign of affection from me as an invitation to screw.

I'd been home for two weeks when I noticed he seemed to be growing more and more edgy. I'd find myself in the middle of an argument with him over something confusedly infuriating and not know how we got there. It all came to a head the afternoon I returned from buying groceries and getting a manicure. He had the dogs out in the vacant lot so they could sniff around and keep a lookout for some human to come along to embrace. He came over to the car to help me carry the groceries into the house.

"Careful, my nails," I said as he took the bag of groceries.

He snatched the bag from me, grabbed the other one from the car, then spun on his heel and stalked toward the house.

I flung my purse strap over my shoulder, called the dogs and followed him into the house.

"What's wrong?" I asked, dropping my purse onto the chair.

Standing stiff-backed in front of a cabinet, putting away groceries, he didn't answer.

"What?"

He stopped. He didn't turn around. "D'you think I'm a fucking moron?" he said.

"Huh?" My mind scrabbled back over what'd I'd said, checking for some unconscious bad attitude on my part. He didn't answer. Instead, he resumed shoving cans of food into the cabinet, then moved over to the fridge.

"Did I miss something?" I said.

Squatting in front of the fridge, he continued unpacking groceries.

"For Godssake, talk to me," I said, raising my voice. "What did I do wrong?"

"You never do anything wrong." He stood, shut the fridge, and turned to face me.

"Well then what happened, just tell me what—"

"I'm tired of being put down."

"Put down? How?"

"What do you always tell me?" He made quotation marks in the air with his fingers. "Intuit it."

I groaned, clenched my fists and brought them up to my temples. "Please don't do this."

"Do what?"

I took a deep breath. "I'm trying to understand here—"

"What's to understand?"

"How you can think I was putting you down."

"Here's another one of your famous quotes: 'If I have to explain it to you . . .'" He let the words hang.

"Goddam it, stop it. Tell me what's going on."

He shook his head like he couldn't believe I could be so stupid.

"What? Don't just shake your head. Talk to me."

He stood there staring at me.

A familiar feeling of desperation took over. "Why do you have to do this whole passive-aggressive thing? Why don't you just come right out and say what's going on?" As usual when we argued, my hands were waving around as I pleaded with him. I stopped when I noticed that his eyes were following my hands, like a little kid watching a puppet show. He'd done this before.

Tears stung my eyes. I let my hands drop to my sides. "Please don't do that."

"Do what?" he asked.

I stamped my foot. "You know what you're doing!"

He stared down at my foot then looked back up at my face. "You're quite the angry little woman, aren't you?"

"You're a fucking asshole." I spun on my heel and headed for the office, slamming our single interior door behind me. The TV blared on.

Sweetpea and Jake padded into the room from the other end of the house. They flopped down on the floor inches from my feet, twin Beanie Babies, white-rimmed eyes pinned on me. I stared down at them, my mind spilling over with desperate, disjointed thoughts. I couldn't do this anymore. I *had* to get out of this marriage. I groaned. No shit. This was *not* making me happy; this was *not* moving me forward. Jake jumped up and retrieved one of the many balls that lay around the house. He dropped it at my feet.

"Not in the house," I muttered. He hunkered down, eyes darting between the ball and my face. Sweetpea's gaze stayed on me. She didn't blink. I ran through a mental litany of what I needed to do to dismantle everything. While he finished fixing the house so we could sell it, I'd have to move to some shitty little apartment in some slum. One that took dogs. One far from work. This whole area had become the Beverly Hills of Orange County and was way too expensive for me to manage on my own. All this crap to sort through. I was going to have to start all over again. I'd worked so hard, I'd saved so hard. And there goes retirement and my full-time writing life. My mind tottered and keeled over. I groaned out loud. Sweetpea sat up, cleared her throat, and lifted her chin with her familiar searching expression. I sank to the floor and hugged her. Jake shoved the ball closer. I threw it across the room. He charged after it.

A few minutes later, I changed into shorts, got Sweetpea and Jake on leashes, put a book on tape in my Walkman, and headed for the hills for a good, long, sweaty hike. Larry was nowhere in sight. Good-bye neighborhood, I thought as I passed familiar houses, neighbors, and their dogs. But I didn't mean it. For the rest of the afternoon and evening, I shied away from any thoughts of the future. I don't think Larry moved from the couch. That night, after punching my pillow a couple of times, I managed to switch off my mind and fall asleep, bookended between Sweetpea and Jake.

The following afternoon, after I got home from work, Larry turned from the sink where he was washing dishes and casually asked if I was over being angry. I studied him for a moment. So completely at ease. Yesterday's incident—its intensity and its implications for our future together—was reduced to a single, potentially passing, problem: my anger. I said something about being sick of his shit. He nodded thoughtfully and told me he shouldn't have gotten pissed off. It was just that he felt I was treating him like he was stupid because he could tell I'd had my nails done.

"So you said," I said. "That's nuts—you know that, don't you?"

"That's what it seemed like to me."

"I just don't get it."

He walked over and took me in his arms. I felt torn; I wanted him to hold me, I wanted to rest there, to be close to him, to pretend everything would work out. But I couldn't. I didn't want to keep going through this. I didn't respond. He lifted my arms, placed them around his waist and held me. I slumped against him and we stood there for a moment.

I looked up at him. "Tell me something. Why do you always let things escalate like that?"

He shrugged. "I was being an asshole."

"But what's with watching my hands like that?"

"I was doing that?"

"Forget it. You're not going to make me feel like I'm going crazy. Sometimes I feel like I'm in that movie, what was it, where the guy dims the lights and does weird things to make his wife think she's going mad."

"I'm the crazy one."

"You like that idea, don't you? Crazy Larry can't help himself. A ticket out of having to deal with anything." I sighed. "Bottom line, you have absolutely no respect for me."

"Sure I do. I respect you more than anyone else in the world."

"You certainly don't act like it," I said. "Doesn't it bother you to see me upset?"

I asked this even though I knew he loved to, in his words, "wind me up." I wished I understood. I could only guess: a diversion from what was bothering him, a way to distance me, a way to feel alive?

True to form, instead of insisting he answer my question, I continued talking. This was how I had always enabled him to evade hard questions, how I avoided facing the truth about our relationship. All he had to do was wait me out. He told me later that's what he'd done his whole life. Just waited everyone out. No need to say anything. I must've been his crowning achievement.

I continued talking until I hit every point I wanted to make and hauled out some old grievances as well. This time I would get through to him; this time he would get it. I could retire on time and pursue a writing life. He didn't move the entire time, his eyes dropping now and then to my mouth like he was reading my lips. When I finally stopped talking, he nodded.

"I'm fucked up, aren't I?"

"That's it?"

"Well, what do you want me to say?"

"I want you to . . ." I stopped. Hadn't we just gone through all that? I shook my head, spun around and headed for the bathroom.

The following Sunday afternoon, we drank beer while we did Sweetpea's treatment. Larry was as adoring toward her as ever. She moved away when he tried to kiss her.

"See, even she doesn't like me," he said, with a rueful grin.

"You've got to be passionate with her," I said. "You know how Staffies are."

"No, she's your dog." He turned to Sweetpea. "Aren't you? I don't blame you. You know the real me, don't you, baby girl? But I don't care. I love you anyway."

I thought about the time Sweetpea kicked him out of bed. She must've stretched; he must've been close to the edge—onto the floor he went. I was awoken by a loud thud and yell and quickly switched on the light.

"She kicked me out of bed!" he cried, peering admiringly at Sweetpea over the edge of the bed from the other side. It was shortly after this that he started sleeping downstairs.

Now I wondered: Why couldn't I have been the one who'd kicked him out of bed?

* * *

Two days later, Layne sent me an email saying he'd successfully moved Garth and Margaret into the Albany. Garth had given his notice to London House management on time. I could just see him marching down West Street in Durban to their offices, dressed in those red suspenders of his, handing over his crudely printed note and then patiently waiting for a receipt. The couple of times I'd spoken on the phone to Garth, he'd told me that he and Margaret were "fine"—his standard response no matter what was going on. I felt at ease only after I confirmed this with Margaret. They had finally moved out of London House.

Eighteen

THAT SATURDAY MORNING I awoke feeling like I was the last person on earth. I had felt this way before, but this particular morning the feeling was more intense than ever. Several times during the past three years I'd crept downstairs to the couch to snuggle up behind Larry. He'd pull my arm over his side and we'd fall asleep, comfortably spooning. But the last time I'd cozied up behind him—this was after the first time he took off for Mexico—he'd awoken with a cranky "What're you doing?" before moving away and pulling the blanket over his shoulders.

Now, as I lay staring up at the ceiling in dawn's faint light, I had the same impulse to slip downstairs. Never in a million years—but still, the urge was there. As if sensing my desperation, Sweetpea raised her head from the pillow—she'd taken over Larry's spot, pillow and all—rolled over, and pawed the air for attention. I kissed her, pulled her close, and spooned with her instead. Jake snuggled up behind me and I fell asleep again.

It was after nine by the time I dragged myself downstairs and into the kitchen. The loneliness had become a dull, aching throb in my chest. It consumed me. This must've been what that guy in the movie *Alien* felt like just before the baby creature burst out of his chest. All I wanted was for Larry to turn back into the man I married: light-hearted, funny, spontaneous, the person with whom I shared my deepest thoughts and who encouraged me when I had doubts.

There was no sign of him. I stiffened and glanced toward the kitchen counter. Another note?

Suddenly he walked through the door and slid his empty plastic bottle, the one he used to wash the saltwater off his body, onto the kitchen counter. He didn't say anything. In the old days, he always walked over to give me a kiss. But this was a more unpredictable man, if that was ever possible: a man who seemed perched on one of those big rubber balls, rolling back and forth, trying to keep his balance. A man who seemed to be poised for something, but who had no idea what that something was.

I walked over and hugged him; I couldn't help it. Tears filled my eyes, words bubbled up and played through my mind, all those words that had already spewed forth five billion times before, angry words, conciliatory words, and all the whys. One more time, let's clear everything up. Let's move on.

He hugged me back. It wasn't any warmer or any longer than his hugs of late had been—God, had it been years since we'd had a good hug?—but in that moment I was so damn needy, it felt good.

"Where've you been?" I chirped.

"Where do you think?"

I pulled back. "What's wrong?"

"Surfing sucked. I suck. I couldn't stand up once. Not once. I don't even know why I bother."

"You're just having a bad day." I leaned back into him.

He shifted from foot to foot. "I've got things to do."

I pulled back; my face felt as if I'd pressed it onto a hot plate.

"Can't you even try?" I said.

He seemed to consider my question, then looked surprised. "Why?"

"Why?" I cried. "Because we're married. Because you keep telling me I haven't done anything wrong. Because you're supposed to love me. Because. Because. Be-fucking-cause."

He stared at me with that hooded look of his. Silence stretched between us.

"Well do you?"

"Do I what?"

"Care about me." The words sounded so damn pathetic. I hated myself for saying them.

"You know I do."

"No, I don't know any such thing. If you loved me you wouldn't take pleasure in goading me, you'd consider my feelings, you'd tell me what's going on. I keep bouncing between hope and hate."

He looked at me as if I'd lost my mind. "You're hopeful?"

"I shouldn't be hopeful?"

"I can't help how you feel," he said, squatting down to stroke Sweetpea.

Rockets burst through my vision. "Goddamn it."

He straightened and considered me for a moment, his face serious. "You've killed my soul."

"What?" I glared at him. "Exactly how?"

"You know what you did."

"I'd love to know what I've done."

"Well, for one thing you've made me sleep downstairs for the past three years, haven't you?" He had that half-amused expression on his face.

I let my head fall back. "Oh, my God, why the fuck would you say—"

"Oh, all right, you didn't make me sleep downstairs."

"Don't. Just don't."

He sighed and shook his head.

I held up my hands. "Okay. I can't do this anymore."

"So then why don't you get a divorce?"

Since the early days of our marriage, he'd thrown this out whenever we had a standoff. "No, I tell you what. Why don't *you* file for divorce? Take responsibility for *something*."

"There you go again, criticizing me."

I pinched my eyes shut then opened them and gave him a brittle smile. "We're in our own little version of Groundhog Day, aren't we?"

The corners of his mouth twitched. "You know you're unhappy."

"Yes, I'm very unhappy." I hated admitting this. It felt like giving up.

"What about your *big* decision?" He made quotation marks in the air with his fingers.

I stared at him. Ah. My blurted confession to him about my dark-night-of-the-soul vows to be happy and to move forward. Why did I always have to tell him everything?

"Fuck if I know," I said wearily. "The pisser is I still care about you."

He was silent for a long moment. "I want out."

It was like he'd stepped out of the fog and hit me across the head with a plank.

"Go ahead and file for divorce," he continued. "You're better at that kind of thing than I am."

Another game? I stared at him. No. He was serious. I couldn't tell if I was devastated or relieved.

"I'm doing you a favor, you know," he said.

No, asshole, you're doing yourself the favor, I wanted to shout. Instead I thought about it. He was right. Barnacle Sandra would never leave otherwise. I nodded. "You are so right."

"I know I am. You're better off without me."

"Right again." I was in uncharted territory. "So, then . . . we'll have to sell the house, of course."

"No, I'll leave," he said. "You can live here, the dogs need a yard."

He couldn't possibly mean it.

"You don't want to leave, do you?" he continued.

"No, of course not." All those times he'd harassed me about leaving.

"Well, then, you should stay. Shouldn't you?"

Just like that.

A crazy normality settled over the rest of the day, as if that little alien in my chest had burst out and squirted me with numbing juice. Larry acted like nothing worth mentioning had happened. Except his bad mood had disappeared. And then, as if discussing where we should holiday next year, we tentatively discussed the logistics of dismantling our marriage. We'd do the divorce ourselves. I would investigate on Monday and also investigate setting up a trust. He'd finish painting the outside of the house and finish up some of the maintenance chores he'd been working on. It vaguely occurred to me that he'd been planning this for some time—all the repairs to the house, getting the garage in order, all those boxes.

He went on to promise that he would babysit Sweetpea and Jake anytime I needed to leave for whatever reason. So helpful and reasonable and direct. We didn't discuss money. I didn't want to think about that part of it. I didn't want to get into what it would mean for us to share ownership of the house, with him coming and going. He wandered off to the garage to work on the Nomad. I paid bills and tried to erase any thoughts of the future from my mind. Later, we drank a couple of beers and I made tacos.

That night, I fell asleep without logging into my inner psychologist. There was nothing to thrash out. My twenty-five-year-old marriage was over.

Nineteen

MONDAY MORNING I awoke earlier than usual. Sweetpea was in her typical spot, head on the pillow, Jake on the other side of her, the bed-clothes in a snarl around my legs. I felt exhausted, yet strangely keyed up. I glanced around my bedroom, almost expecting to find myself in some unfamiliar place. Outside, a gust of wind sent the somber peal of the big Soleri bell echoing through the house. Sweetpea stirred and pressed her broad snout against my cheek, hard, like I might be leaving on a trip. I snuggled up to her and fell back asleep.

Half an hour later, I stretched and then lay staring up at the ceiling. What now? Where would he go? How would he manage? Would I be able to get by without his income? I arose and started downstairs, this time doing Larry's cautious sideways crawl instead of my customary hop and skip.

I glanced into the living room. Empty. Had he gone surfing? Sweet-pea and Jake clicked alongside me and looked up expectantly. When I opened the front door they charged past me and dashed toward the stand of bamboo in front of the studio. A family of raccoons had set up house there for the winter. I heard the dogs give a couple of barks and scuffle around, no doubt straining up at the thick bamboo stalks where they'd last caught sight of one of the creatures.

I sank down onto the front step and gazed across the deck in the early morning light, looking at the wooden shelving Larry had strung from one end of the deck to the other—two wide planks filled with a myriad of plants, most of them in pots he'd made: that little cacti dangling a slender spiked tail that turned up at the end, a South African elephant's foot cactus, a couple of Bonsai pines, and a heart-shaped hoya I'd fancied as a symbol of our love.

I thought of all the little treasures Larry had surreptitiously slipped into spots throughout the yard: the cracked four-inch ceramic elf-man I'd made and he'd rescued, kneeling serenely in a rotted section of an upright railroad tie; a small, rubber toy dragon he'd found while delivering mail snuggled in a knothole in the fence; a tarnished, one-square-inch brass tag proclaiming "Dirty Old Man" nailed under the eaves near the front door. I was always finding some little gem, sometimes years after he'd hidden them. "You're not very observant, are you?" he'd say.

To my right sat the three kilns we'd acquired to fire our wares: his thrown pots and my hand-built ceramic fish, porcelain lilies, jars, and wall hangings. I thought about all those years we sold our merchandise at the Sawdust Festival and the Westwood Street Fair, how much fun that had been. This was mostly during the summer months, when we'd spent eighteen-hour days side by side, designing, creating, experimenting with glazes, and then firing and selling our wares before and after work at the post office.

After four years we gave it all up. I'd hurt my back at work, and his already gimpy shoulder had worsened. I started writing and he continued to subscribe to *Ceramics Monthly*, with the intent to return to the craft full-time when he retired and didn't have the pressure of working as well. But that hadn't happened. He'd lost interest. I was about to be alone. I sighed. Across the canyon, the sun struggled up through a pack of grey clouds. I sat and watched until it broke through, then hurried back into the house to dress for work.

The note was in the same place as before, on the counter next to the stove. "Gone to Mexico to build my adobe house and to look for some warm water. Don't forget to feed the fish." A joking reference to my comment that he should build his own little adobe house down in

Mexico as an alternative to living in his van. It felt like someone had slipped a piano wire noose around my neck and yanked me sideways. Why did I expect anything else?

The *Alien* baby was back in my chest, curled into a tight ball. I wanted to jump in the car and head for parts unknown. Away from the scene of the crime, from my life. And my job, where I was due to appear in the next hour. How could I possibly deal with what was happening there in light of what was unfolding here in my house?

Downsizing was depressing for everyone at work, but now I was the one issuing life-changing letters to people I cared about. And from the looks of things, I was in line for one of those letters myself. My job was being slowly absorbed by a remote, centralized system that required employees to make personnel changes via either computer or telephone. And now, with the divorce, I no longer had the luxury of retiring early, as I had planned, or even retiring at all, at least for a long time.

But I just couldn't bring myself to play hooky. It was the last day of "Open Season" for medical benefits, including the chance to switch savings plans. I had to be there. Those employees who didn't have a computer or who lacked the skills to negotiate the fledgling system or who had trouble communicating in their broken English turned to me for help. I'd been admonished by higher-ups at the call center for coddling employees, but I didn't care.

The moment I entered the building, I felt like Princess Leia in *Star Wars*—the first one, where she and Luke Skywalker are trapped and the walls and roof of the spaceship are closing in on them. Taking a deep breath, I started down the pathway behind the carrier cases toward my office at the front of the building.

"Hey, how's that Lar-dog doing?" a familiar voice called from behind the cases. It was one of the guys who'd worked with us in the old days. I got this question every now and then.

"Oh, just terrific," I called back.

Knowing laughs.

A hand gripped my arm. "Sandrita, please, you must help me."

I turned. It was Rosa. Falling into step beside me, she continued, "I get mixed up and the computer tells me I have no more chances, it is too late, and the stock market it is so bad, oh, Sandrita, I will lose all my *money*." The last word came out in a wail.

Glancing over my shoulder for her supervisor, I slipped my arm around her shoulders. "Come, let's go fix this for you." I hurried her toward my office before the supervisor noticed she was missing. These days employees were expected to make personnel changes off the clock.

It took me half an hour to guide her through a two-minute process. I forgot my problems. By now heads were poking in and out of my office: employees charging back and forth from their jobs—some on break, some not—to be next in line. Rosa finally left and Dan Chong, shooting daggers at her, shot in with his monthly gift of a jar of kim chee, big enough to feed a family of five for two weeks.

"You are *too* patient," he cried and held out the jar.

"Actually, I'm not," I said, eyeing him. He seemed more agitated than usual. I rose from behind my desk and took the jar. "You don't have to do this, you know, I'll help you for free."

"You need kim chee!"

"You're right. I do. Now more than ever." I grinned; this was our usual routine. I'd learned not to chastise him for spending his money on me. He loved that I loved the smelly Korean cabbage delicacy. When he left, I'd quickly smuggle the jar out to my car so it didn't stink up the office. "You're a good man, Dan Chong. Okay, so what's up?"

Turned out his wife, who worked for the Postal Service in another office, had received a letter: she was to be transferred to an office fifty miles away, along one of the most congested freeways in the USA. She was eligible to retire, but she needed more time to get full retirement. He was in the same boat. But she was going to call it quits, and she expected him to do the same—she had already filed his retirement papers, along with hers. They were to move to North Dakota, where they would live with their physician daughter and her husband in order to babysit their eighteen-month-old granddaughter. This is what Korean parents did. But Dan wasn't ready to go; his job was safe, he liked what he did, he didn't want to leave his church and all his friends, Dakota was too cold, his wife "in too much hurry."

"What must I do?" he moaned, clutching his head.

I knew it was a rhetorical question. He would go, of course; it was the Korean way. "Family is all," he'd told me many times.

"Don't go," I said. Everyone was leaving. Things were changing too fast. "Who will bring me kim chee?"

He didn't answer; instead, he threw back his head in a short, barking laugh and then nodded thoughtfully, regret written all over his face.

"Write and let me know how you're doing, okay?"

He laughed again and looked uncomfortable. I knew he wouldn't. He just wasn't the type to keep in touch. I saw him one more time—from a distance, on the workroom floor—and then he was gone from my life.

I returned home that afternoon to find Larry's boxes of T-shirts gone from the garage, along with the beer boxes he'd filled with odds and ends. No doubt he'd packed them in the VW the night before. I stared at the empty spaces feeling as if I'd just discovered a robbery, as if I'd been violated in some way. It was his stuff, after all. This was the way he did things. Damn him.

Later that evening, I went online to research do-it-yourself divorces and trusts. I wrestled with whether to get a lawyer or not. But according to my research a lawyer didn't seem necessary. With our circumstances, the whole process was pretty much cut-and-dried. He wanted out; he wanted to cut loose from everything in his life—me, his family, the house, and Southern California. I didn't believe it was in his nature to pull a fast one if something went wrong with the paperwork. That would be too much trouble.

Within three hours I'd discovered a company recommended by consumer advocate Dave Horowitz. Divorce and trust paperwork would arrive within the week. Well, that was that. I was about to become a two-time loser.

* * *

Two days later, Layne called from South Africa.

"Mom," he began in a hesitant voice.

"Layne?"

"It's Garth."

"What's wrong?"

"He had a stroke."

Clutching the phone until my hand hurt, I bombarded Layne with questions, but he couldn't tell me much. Two days earlier he'd received a call from a Deon, a friend of Margaret's, who'd phoned from Addington hospital in Durban. Garth had been taken there after collapsing in his room at the Albany as he dressed for work.

For the past two days Layne had been trying to gather information about Garth's condition, but what with South Africa's recent problems with cell phone transmission—anything from loud crackling to cut-off calls—he hadn't been able to learn much. Deon's monosyllabic answers in a thick Afrikaans accent didn't help. And he was unable to get any information out of the beleaguered doctors, who usually worked in privately-owned hospitals but were required to work extra shifts in government-owned ones like Addington. Layne wanted to drive down to Durban, but Deon had persuaded him to wait a couple more days. Layne promised to keep me posted.

I sank to the floor. So much for a better life for my brother. I'd have to return to South Africa to take care of him. I would have to take out a loan. A second mortgage on the house? How would that work with the divorce? What about the dogs? And who was this Deon? My poor little brother, in the hands of strangers. The following morning I told my boss I would probably be returning to South Africa soon to check on my brother. I had the vacation time. It shouldn't be a problem, he said, and wished me well.

In subsequent phone calls over the next two days, Layne urged me to stay put until he gathered more information. I would be in the way, he said. Five days later we finally received information about Garth's condition. Turned out his right side was partially paralyzed, his speech slightly slurred. According to Deon, he had a chance of recovering most of his mobility with physical therapy.

Layne also learned that Deon was actually *Leon*, a friend of Margaret's stepsister Sheila; he lived behind Sheila's house in Hillary, twenty-five miles north of Durban. I knew about Sheila from Garth. Over the years she had taken Margaret over to her house now and then for a weekend. She worked for the South African version of the Veteran's Administration, which is where she had procured Margaret's wheelchair. She also already rented a room to Marie, a seventy-seven-year-old retiree.

By now Leon had taken Garth to Sheila's house, where she was taking care of him. Leon eventually took Margaret to Sheila's as well, where she and Garth shared a room until other arrangements could be made. Meanwhile, Social Services provided periodic physical therapy for Garth.

"Agh man, we must help where we can," Leon said after Layne's third offer to pay for Garth's care. "Besides, he doesn't eat much."

A couple of days later, I finally managed to speak to Garth. He told me matter-of-factly that he'd had a stroke but was coming along nicely. The sound of his faint voice filled me with a profound sadness. The following day I deposited money into Garth's bank account, then called Leon and Company to tell them to take the money they needed. Ultimately they withdrew money to cover Garth's physical therapy, and nothing more.

Layne set about researching what South Africa calls Frail Care Homes, which provides accommodation and nursing for those in need—something like assisted living in the States. Meanwhile, he and Irma had started building the house they'd mentioned when I was in South Africa. I'd seen tentative plans that involved a suite for me—for my inevitable return "home." Maybe now they'd need a room for Garth.

Despite Layne's admonitions, I felt compelled to hop on a plane to South Africa. Two weeks after the stroke, however, Layne continued to urge me to wait and see.

I called Garth.

In a voice slightly stronger than before, he told me he was fine, except for Sheila's continual nagging for him to eat his vegetables and to drink lots of water. She was also making him take a little walk every day, just down the street to the corner and back again.

"Do you go by yourself?"

"Ja," he said, drawing out the word questioningly like I was nuts for asking him something like that.

"So what else do you do, then?"

"I watch television with them."

"What's your favorite show?"

"*One Life to Live*. It's American."

"They have that show there?"

"Ja. It's Sheila's favorite."

"Listen, can I do anything for you, send you anything? Maybe some Cheetos?" I knew how much he loved the cheesy snack.

"Too much cholesterol."

"You're right, of course, what was I thinking?"

"Ja," he said, a smile in his voice. "Bad for my heart. But I would like some more CDs."

"Of course. But listen, I can't get any more Jim Reeves for you. We bought out the shop." I'd actually found the American country singer Garth had adopted when my mother fell in love with him back in the fifties through mail order. "Shall I just see what other old-time 'cowboy' singers I can find and send those?"

"Ja."

"I love you."

"Ja."

We hung up and I sank into a chair and stared up at the ceiling. Garth's needs were so simple; porridge with a dab of butter and a sprinkling of sugar in the morning, some kind of meat sandwich on buttered bread at noon, a cup of tea with milk and sugar twice a day, meat and potatoes at night, and a beer now and then. And his music. At least the stroke hadn't diminished his passion for that.

I could almost feel his hand in the small of my back guiding me through the parking garage that day after I tripped, making sure I gripped the escalator railing as we headed to the second floor of the mall. Layne was right. I should just plan on returning in April as planned, when we could all spend some quality time together. Meanwhile, I had the divorce to complete.

* * *

During Garth's crisis I'd received the divorce and trust paperwork in the mail, but with so much on my mind I'd simply plunked the package at the far end of the dining room table, next to the car magazines that had arrived in the mail for Larry. I'd felt adrift and vulnerable, unable to deal with the end of my marriage as well as Garth's stroke. Now I retrieved the package and stared down at it. What if I needed Larry's input on questions I didn't know the answers to? And, of course, I'd need his signature once I got through everything. What if he didn't come back?

It struck me that I didn't want him to return. Life was so much simpler without him. In the beginning I'd missed having someone with whom to share the distress of Garth's stroke, the advent of the baby hawk in the vacant lot learning to fly, and the travesty of Deidrich's Coffee on Coast Highway being replaced by yet another Starbuck's just five hundred yards from the other Starbuck's opposite Main Beach. I'd also missed the way he helped me cut through the bullshit when I got lost in doubt about issues at work. That particular version of Larry was usually present and insightful and helpful. But then I realized that other than the anguish over Garth's condition, I hadn't been feeling as charged up when I tried to sleep—"nervy," I called it, when I couldn't lay still, like the bed was rigged to shock me every few minutes. I'd been sleeping through the night. The little alien in my chest had disappeared.

I positioned the paperwork at the head of the table, poured myself a glass of wine, retrieved a pen, and settled down to take care of business. I read the first page of the divorce. It was simple enough. At first. But with each successive page I felt myself sinking deeper into a bog of legalese. My mind slipped over the words. I had to read through each sentence two or three times to comprehend the information. I gave up halfway through and skimmed the trust. It was worse. I'd have to try again some other time.

Three days later, I rushed home at lunchtime to let out the dogs. The forecast had called for rain, so I'd left them in the house. When I opened the gate I noticed that the front door stood ajar. Had I failed to shut it properly this morning? I threw a panicked glance at the pond, momentarily terrified of finding both Sweetpea and Jake's bodies floating on the surface. Jake burst from behind the door, followed by Sweetpea, followed a moment later by Larry, who blinked like he'd just woken from a nap.

"You're home *very* early," he said.

Like the time I came home early to spend the afternoon with you and walked in on you and your girlfriend seven years after the affair? The words popped into my head before I could stop them, along with a red tide of anger. Anger over the recollection of that horrible day; anger over the cowardly way he'd tried to distract me; anger over the taunting, singsong voice he used now. Sweetpea and Jake barreled into me. I bent down to hug them, trying to gather myself.

"I've been coming home at lunchtime to let the dogs out to pee," I said, trying to keep my voice even. He would not feed on my anger today.

"*Every* day?"

"No," I said rising to my feet. "Only when I keep them inside because of the weather, otherwise I leave them outside."

He frowned. "You leave them outside?"

"Yes. I leave them outside. Like we used to when both of us worked?"

He nodded as if losing interest in the conversation. "Did you finish the divorce?"

"I'm working on it."

"Still?"

"Yes. Still. I don't see you working on it."

"You said you'd take care of it."

In a flash, the distance I'd gained with his absence disappeared. I couldn't stop myself. "No, you cold-hearted, irresponsible dick, you said I'd take care of it."

"I don't call you names."

This gave me pause. I'd always worked so hard not to call him names. It always meant another detour. Plus, I didn't want to weaken my position of being the wronged one. But underneath it all, I realized, I still had a ghost of a fear that I hadn't done everything to make the marriage work. How fucking pathetic, I thought and headed back toward the gate; I had to return to work.

I returned home later that afternoon to find him on the couch watching Gunsmoke. He stayed there for the next two days with the lights off, mostly watching old Westerns or slowly switching from station to station. I asked him to please turn down the TV. He obliged. Other than that, I didn't feel compelled to deal with him. We were on a short track to the end. I went back to restless, sleepless nights. I worked on the divorce and trust. And then on the third day, when I returned from an after-work hike up the hill, he looked up from the TV and told me that Layne had called.

I peered into the darkened room. "You answered the phone?"

"Why didn't you tell me Garth had a stroke?"

"What do you care?" I said, knowing how childish the words sounded.

"Well, I do."

"So what did Layne say?"

"He found a place called Settler's or something like that." He pulled a slip of paper from his pocket and squinted down at it. "Yeah, Settler's, it's a Frail Care something or other."

"That's it?"

"Pretty much."

"He didn't fill you in on what happened to Garth, ask you how you are, how I am? What was going on?" I knew Layne would've chatted away. Despite everything, he cared about his stepfather, considered him family.

"Well, yeah."

I shook my head. "It's like pulling frickin' teeth with you trying to get more than the bare essentials, isn't it?"

"We're not all like you, Sandra."

"That's too bad, isn't it?"

He grinned. "Yes, it is, actually. No, it really is. So, what's been going on?"

It was like he'd flipped a switch. He'd never been gone, we weren't getting a divorce. But we were. It was over. What did I have to lose? I sank into the rocking chair opposite him. I told him my concerns about Garth. I told him how I'd wanted to fly back to South Africa to be with Garth, a good clean feeling of just wanting to be there for him, not my old guilt-soaked compulsion. I told him I wanted to be able to fly to South Africa at a moment's notice. He reminded me he'd agreed to babysit the dogs anytime; all I had to do was ask. And whatever money Garth needed, I should take it from our savings account. He also assured me that everything would work out for Garth.

"What color is the sky in your world?" I said.

"What, now?"

"How can you be so nice, so supportive, just like that, after . . . I . . . I just don't get it." But I did get it; he cared when there were no personal emotional stakes.

"What, I shouldn't want to help you? Do you want me to be an asshole?"

"No, of course not."

"Say it." He grinned. "Go on . . . Why change now?"

I gave him a wry grin, rose, and headed for the kitchen. "Hungry?"

"You don't have to cook for me," he called back.

"Oh, what the hell, I'm making something for myself, might as well make something for the asshole."

"Calling me names, again," he called back without rancor.

Later we had dinner in front of the TV. But something had definitely shifted in me: no buds of hope, no wondering what he had planned, what this all meant. Instead I felt light, focused on the moment.

Twenty

I CALLED LAYNE the following afternoon after work.

"Hello," his sleepy voice crackled across the line.

I glanced at the clock. "Oops," I said. "Forgot about the time difference. Sorry."

"Payback's a bitch," he said, teasing. All those times he used to call me at all hours when he first got to South Africa.

"Funny how that works out, hey?" I said laughing. "Real quick, you found a place for Garth?"

"Well, yes, and no. It's a long story."

"Okay, an email tomorrow, then?"

"Will do," he said through a yawn. "It's halfway written anyway."

"Loveyoubye."

"Loveyoubye."

The following morning, a Saturday, I found a glass of orange juice waiting for me on the counter; Larry had gone to the Pomona Swap Meet and Classic Car Show. I'd always welcomed a moment like this—an overture on his part, an indication that we were good again. But this time it was different. We had business to conduct.

That afternoon I read Layne's email. He'd arranged to visit Garth before heading over to Settler's. He sat elbow-to-elbow in the front room of Sheila's small brick house, built "circa 1888," as the sign said—the oldest in Hillary—along with Sheila, Leon, Margaret, Garth, and Marie, drinking tea and eating Marie's melktert. From his description I could just see Sheila, small and wiry, probably in her sixties, with the squint and rasp of an ex-smoker and a Dust Bowl gaze. After her husband died she'd retired and begun renting out her two extra rooms to retirees, both for the company and a little extra cash.

Across a sparse lawn in back sat Leon's one-bedroom house. Turned out Leon owned a small nursery down the street and rented out his own house in order to "keep an eye" on the women. In the front yard, a small metal sign stuck in the rich red dirt of a flower bed alongside a path to the door proclaimed "Beware! Cranky Old Women."

"Mom," Layne wrote in his e-mail, "these are, how do you say, 'salt of the earth people.'" They tell me this story, how they'd been asking Garth if they could make him something special to eat because all he'd been eating was a piece of toast and little else. So this one morning he gets up and tells them, 'A spot of roast beef would be nice.' Just like that. They laughed about it. I think he got his roast beef. I didn't ask." Layne went on to say that the visit to Settler's Home didn't go well. "The place was like something out of the nineteenth century," he wrote. "You know those insane asylums you see in movies? Anyway, Leon said not to worry—Garth can stay until we find a place. I'll keep looking. Garth's physical therapy is coming along nicely."

Larry returned later that afternoon. We stood in the kitchen while he told me about all the cars he'd seen, including that green '37 slant-back Ford he'd liked so much at the Long Beach Car Show a year ago. Did I remember it? I did. He told me how he got lost again getting there. Like we always did when we went together.

"So did you have a beer and a steak sandwich?" I asked.

"I had a beer—actually, I had a couple. I almost didn't, at seven dollars apiece. But no sandwich." He gave me one of his fakey sappy looks. "It just wouldn't have been the same without you."

"Or was it just getting too expensive at that point?"

He grinned. "Kinda."

"By the way, where's the VW? And your T-shirts and whatever else was in those boxes you sneaked away?"

"What do you mean?"

"I'm just curious. It's not a hard question."

"I didn't sneak anything away. It's my stuff."

"I don't care what you took. It's just the way you did it. So where did it end up?"

"In Mexico."

"Nice. A direct answer. So T-shirts are in the VW in Mexico?" He cocked his head and gave me an amused look. "Uh-huh."

"We're getting somewhere."

"Anything else you want to know?"

"Can I go get my list?" I made as if to bolt for my storehouse of questions.

"Okay, okay," he said, holding up his hands. "You can ask away later. Let's take care of the divorce first."

I gathered the folder I'd created and headed for the study, where he waited cross-legged on the floor. Sweetpea and Jake trotted in behind me then sprawled on either side of us as I settled down opposite him. I'd managed to plough through the bulk of both the divorce and trust papers, completing the sections titled "Schedule of Assets and Debts," "Income and Expense Declaration," and "Community and Quasi-Community Property Declaration." I'd filled out most of his part, too, like I usually did with all our business and legal matters.

I explained what I'd done, asked him to check over everything—he declined, saying he trusted me—and had him fill out those portions of his information I wasn't sure about. Because neither of us would be contesting the divorce, the paperwork was less complicated than it might have otherwise been. The trust took a little longer. For the first time in years, he remained engaged in our interaction for longer than ten minutes, even going so far as to help me find the paperwork we needed on the house.

He'd meant what he said about me staying in the house. I felt a profound relief about this. It would make my life so much easier. And I knew him well enough to know that he'd given this a lot of thought. This was a man who loved his things, someone who repaired broken pots and vases that were way beyond saving because of his attachment to them. He wanted out badly enough to give up all of it.

We agreed that I would live in the house until such time that I wanted to sell, in which case he would get half the proceeds. If I died, he could either move back or sell; if he chose to sell, his kids and mine would get their equal share. I listened in amazement as he told me that he was going to leave everything he'd brought into the marriage, including all his parents' effects: cutlery, crockery, quilts, photos, childhood memorabilia, his father's antique safe and BB gun, his grandmother's valuable antique glassware and teacups, and family photos, as well as all the furniture, artwork and ceramics we'd accumulated together—the Akita-sized metal dragonfly we'd bought in Santa Monica, the three giant antique Chinese jars, the rare Japanese prints and cloisonné jars. All of it would remain with the house. The kids could fight over it later, is how he put it. He'd keep the VW and van, and I would get the 2002 Nissan Altima. "Screwed again," he joked. "I get the old clunkers and you get the new car." The Nomad would stay where it was for now, although he did offer to store it if I wanted to park the Altima in the garage. Either way, it was half mine.

I wondered if he would regret any of these arrangements later. But then I remembered something his dad once said—that in the end, Larry always did whatever he wanted to do. I thought of all those insane conversations when I'd beg him to stop teasing me or hounding me for sex, and he'd say, Why can't you just let me be me?

"So don't be selling everything as soon as I leave," he said with a crooked grin.

By now I was lying on my side, head propped on my hand, snug in our bonhomie. "Hey, I'm not your ex," I said, grinning back. She had sold their belongings the five different times she left him.

"It's a wonder I had anything left after she was done."

"You know how to pick 'em, all right."

"I got better at it."

"Oh, so, you've already got someone better lined—"

"No," he said, frowning. "I mean you. Marrying you is still the best thing I ever did."

My heart stumbled. I stared at him. He was as good-looking as ever, even with his long white and thinning hair—that full mouth, that same crooked bottom tooth I wanted to tongue, that deep seductive air of calm and confidence. He'd said those words for the first time two years after we married. It was one night after a co-worker's wedding; we ditched our friends and screwed on the beach in San Clemente, then sat talking until dawn. He ruminated about not meeting me sooner, how much further along we could've been financially, how his and my children could've been our children, how he wished we could've had a baby together (he'd had a vasectomy). He'd gone on about how he'd always taken the easy way out. But now he had me. I called him on his bullshit, is what he said. Now he had a chance at living the life he'd always wanted.

"You know, I used to believe that marrying you was the best thing I ever did, too."

He gave me a fake double-take, then shrugged. "You know something? You give everyone *way* too much credit."

"Yeah?"

"Everybody. Me. Especially me. I'm an asshole."

"What have I been saying all—"

"And then there are my kids. All the problems, you know? They . . . I don't know. There's always something. I mean with a mother like my ex and a father like me, what do you expect? Right? I mean I love them and all, but I must not have the dad gene. I wish I felt differently. I wish I knew how to deal with it all. It makes me feel really bad. But I just don't. It must come from my dad. He was a great guy and everything. But he was never there. *There.* Making me do things. Disciplining me, taking any kind of stand. He never taught me things. Like he never let me help him fix the car. He never showed me *how* to do it, didn't explain what it was he was doing. I just stood there holding the tools, watching him. He just did everything himself. I don't remember him ever talking to me. Really talking to me." He shook his head and waved a hand like he'd gone too far.

A hundred words bubbled up. You can change. Start now. I'll help you. But we'd had this conversation before, too many times. I plucked at the paperwork at my feet.

He rose to his feet. "Want a beer?"

"Sure." I stared out the window while he headed toward the kitchen. So many years of struggling, first with our respective kids, and then without the kids. How differently everything had turned out than I'd hoped.

I thought about Darin and Layne, the gut-wrenching, heart-stomping turmoil and guilt I went through after John kicked them out and they moved in with us. I constantly felt at a loss, unsure where to draw the line, especially since Larry left me alone in the middle of the conflicts, making me responsible for everything they did wrong, never once confronting them or the issues. Still, I kept looking to him for help. I had been the eternal optimist, but in the end I was merely an accomplice to his refusal to take responsibility. He was right; I *had* given him way too much credit. More accurately, I had expected him to be more than he was willing or capable of being. What it got me was a warehouse of resentment that would eventually rupture, get patched up, and then burst again. Had I let my sons down? Perhaps. But at least Layne thought I was wise—and even Darin, heir apparent to John's throne of uptightness, once told me, "At least I have part of you in me."

Larry returned and handed me a beer, then clinked his bottle against mine. "Here's to you."

"And you." I took a sip. "So where are you going to live?"

"I don't know."

"You're just going to wander around until you decide?"

"Probably."

I took another sip and set the bottle down. "That's no answer."

"God, you're relentless. Yes, I'm going to wander around."

"What about Mexico?"

"It's getting too dangerous down there."

I shook my head and considered him for a moment. "Do you know what you're doing?"

He gave a lopsided grin. "No."

I nodded and stared down at the floor, torn between pity and futility. Wandering around by himself. A little dot in an unending landscape.

"You're not going to figure this one out," he said. "So give it up."

"Do you think I can do that?"

He grinned. "Probably not." He leaned forward, lifted my chin and kissed me. Soft and loving. He shifted closer; his hand came up ready to cup my breast. I jerked back.

"Come onnn," I said. "Do you think I'm a complete idiot?"

"No," he said softly, leaned forward and kissed me again, no hand this time. I started to pull back but then felt myself sinking into an eternal moment filled with his warmth, his core stillness, his male musk, the ripeness of his lips, years of wanting him: gentle, sweet. By the time he cupped my breast again, I had forgotten how for all those years his jabbing and tweaking my breasts had been some kind of twisted mix of lust and love. A tiny voice in the background screamed *What the hell am I doing?* I ignored it and allowed the moment to carry me on a wave of desire and intimacy. And then, still kissing, we wriggled out of our clothes and stretched out on the floor. His erection lasted no more than one minute. We writhed desperately, to no avail. I rubbed and coaxed and kissed. Sounds of frustration from him. Sweetpea thrust her head between our faces. Jake sniffed Larry's butt and it was all over.

He fell over onto his back. We laughed. I stretched out and stared up at the ceiling.

He stroked my stomach. "I'm useless."

I patted his hand. "You really should get a physical."

"Why?"

"Don't give me that shit that you don't mind dying."

Jake rushed over and licked my face with his usual maniacal intensity. I covered my face with both hands. Jake turned to Larry, who allowed a few licks and then did the same. Giving up, Jake wedged his body between us and curled into a ball. Sweetpea stared down at me, her nose inches from mine. I patted her, got up, and pulled on my pants.

Larry rose to his feet, gave me a hug, and then bent down to pick up his pants. "Sorry about Rootie here." He sneaked a reproachful glance down at his penis.

I grinned. "Haven't heard that in a while."

He reached for me. "We could try again."

"Um, I don't think so," I said, moving out of his reach.

He nodded.

"So, where were we?" I sank back down onto the floor and pulled the divorce paperwork toward me.

He bent over and lifted my chin. "I really do care about you."

He never did tell me what he would be taking. I'd find out later, after he was gone. We finished up what we could with the business at hand. There were a few other items to work through and then all that remained was to get everything notarized. He told me he would finish painting the outside of the house and complete the room that was to have been his studio. He would also babysit Sweetpea and Jake while I visited Darin and his family in Davis in two months, and any other time

I needed him. And he would always be available to help with any major repairs that needed to be done to the house or the pond.

In the waning light of the afternoon, we gathered all the paperwork together and set it on the dining room table. Then we headed outside, where he showed me how to turn off the gas and water heater, how to clean the pond filter, and how to replace it, and asked would I please start the Nomad every three weeks or so to keep it running? He got us another beer while I headed into the kitchen to start dinner. It felt almost as if he was just going on a long vacation, taking a break.

"I'm going to leave soon," he said. "I've got to find a place to live."

"When?"

He shrugged. "I'm not sure yet, I want to go up to Mavericks tomorrow for a couple of days." Mavericks: famous "radical" surf spot at Half Moon Bay in Northern California with waves that can crest over sixty feet in frigid waters, dangerous currents, jagged rocks, and the ever-present threat of the Great White Shark.

"Mavericks?" I said, reaching for the wok. "Isn't that where that surfer—what was his name—got killed?"

"Mark Foo."

"You hate to surf waves any bigger than head-high." I placed the wok on the stove and started chopping green onions.

"Not anymore."

I shot a glance at him. Was this some kind of death wish? I dismissed the thought.

The rest of the night passed in the routine we'd established over the years, minus the tension, and then I went upstairs to bed while he remained on the couch and continued to watch TV. Sweetpea and Jake followed me upstairs. I settled in between them and stared up at the ceiling in the shifting light of the TV playing through the leaded glass window in the wall. The volume was turned to its usual blare.

Twenty-one

AS I ROUNDED the corner the following afternoon on my way home from work, my heart sank when I saw that the van was gone. I parked the Altima and sat staring through the front window at the lush green carpet of weeds that had sprung up in the vacant lot over the past couple of months. Spring was already here. The bamboo behind me rustled. That damned bamboo that buckled the asphalt in front of the house and whose roots made planting anything anywhere in the yard a pickaxe operation. It was now my responsibility to keep it under control. Who the hell plants enough bamboo to cover a small principality around a Hobbit-sized yard? I sighed. A man who wanted to keep the world out. I scrambled from the car, suddenly anxious to see Sweets and Jake. I needed some love.

"I saw Larry pull out with a surfboard this morning," a voice behind me said. It was the neighbor from across the street. He was getting into his truck. He glanced in the Altima's backseat, where I had a stack of empty boxes for my soon-to-be ex-husband's move. "Must be nice taking off any old time."

I managed a rueful grin. "Must be." Probably his wife had shared with him the details of Larry's frequent disappearances. I hadn't been able to bring myself to tell her about the divorce. Was I holding onto the hope that everything would work out in the end?

"Back to Mexico?" He started his truck.

"Mavericks," I said.

"Whoa. Aren't those waves a little big for him?"

"He's just going to check them out," I said, grabbing my purse from the passenger seat. A shiver of unease ran down my spine. "Pee-wee's latest adventure."

He laughed and started forward. "Well, see you later."

I thought back to the conversation I'd had with that neighbor down the street who called Larry a "vortex" for his ability to draw in, even mesmerize, her and her husband with his off-the-wall humor and talent for hanging on to every word. During one of his absences, she shouted out how much she missed him as she drove by. Another time she stopped and, with her expression crumbling, told me how sorry she was. "I hadn't realized . . ." she said.

"Oh, it's okay," I said, feeling bad for her, embarrassed for me. "I'm all right." Her husband later told me, his eyes moist, about a friend of his who'd been depressed and committed suicide. Larry, it seemed, had become another wayward soul to them.

I headed for the gate. I wondered if Larry had shared any of his plans, or the turmoil he was going through with *anyone*. I couldn't imagine it. Mr. I-don't-have-any-friends—"Well, except for you," he'd say. And her. The only other person he'd ever called "friend." Did she somehow fit into the picture? The thought unnerved me. I'd recently learned that she'd moved to Oregon three years earlier. Had Larry been in contact with her all this time? Could he really be that deceptive? I put the idea out of my mind. We were getting a divorce; why was I still beating that dead donkey? The rest of the afternoon and evening passed in a blur of routine.

Four days later, Larry pulled into the vacant lot next to the house just as I returned from work. I resisted hugging him. He hadn't killed himself. But it didn't take long before we were in one of our classic go-rounds, me asking him to explain something he'd just said, him repeating the exact same words in his usual deadpan way, me flipping out, followed by a feeling of futility.

"See," he said. "This is why I have to leave, we just don't get along."

For the next week I worked hard to avoid getting lured back into his games. He alternated between working on the house and packing his clothes into the empty copy paper boxes I'd brought from work. These included the Reyn Spooner surf shirts and semi-dress pants he hadn't worn for years, his leather "dress" flip-flops, a pair of Birkenstocks, Wallabies, Van's tennies and those huaraches we'd gotten in Mexico that one time. Then there were the rest of his T-shirts: the ones with logos from the Sawdust Festival, art and car shows, surf trips to Costa Rica and Jeffrey's Bay, South Africa. Soon these day-to-day reminders of our shared experiences would be gone. With each filled box that appeared in the garage, another space loomed in the house, along with a quiver in my center.

I helped him wrestle the last two eight-by-twelve-inch fascia planks into place in front of the peaked studio roof, him purple-faced atop an eight-foot-high ladder while I wobbled below, toting the heavy beam up to him on tippy toes from a shorter ladder. Old times. And then there was the top to the raku kiln, an octagonal, wagon-wheel-sized cap of firebrick and metal, heavy as a house, that we lugged bent-kneed from the corner of the yard to the deck. He didn't need help with the rest of the kiln; it could be moved brick by brick. I didn't ask him why the thing needed moving.

The following day I returned home to find the dishes done and the kitchen floor swept. This time the note stuck halfway out from beneath the toaster where it had drifted when I slapped down my notebook.

"I put $1,500 in checking. Hope it covers everything. See you in two months to babysit Sweetpea and Jake. Take care of them. Love you."

A dam inside me broke. Before I knew it, I was bawling: big, chest-heaving sobs. I stood there with my hands covering my face. I couldn't stop long enough to reach for a paper towel right by my elbow. And then it was like I was watching a video: Larry driving down the coast at his usual forty-five miles per hour, the newly painted van packed to the roof with boxes and brown paper bags stuffed with his clothes, both hands on the steering wheel, eyes straight ahead, wisps of long white hair lifting in the breeze from the half-open window. He clutches the gearshift and gently, effortlessly shifts into third gear, something I've never been able to do.

I felt the prick of Sweetpea and Jake's twin laser gazes. They'd already jumped up on me once, but I hadn't realized it at the time. I grabbed a wad of paper towels, wiped my face and blew my nose. A couple more shudders rippled through me.

"Yeah, I know," I said, bending down to kiss each dog on the snout. "What the hell am I crying for? I'm moving forward, for God's sake." I straightened. "Okay, so enough of that."

They stared expectantly up me.

"I suppose you two want to go for a . . ." I paused for dramatic effect and then, forcing myself, yelled, "Walk!"

They outdid each other, spinning and charging back and forth toward the drawer, before grasping the collars and leashes in their teeth. I grinned. They made me happy. Five minutes later we headed down the canyon toward the beach.

* * *

For the next week I moved through life in a mindless limbo. The divorce and trust papers still lay on the dining room table where I'd tidied them into neat piles; paper clips marked all the areas I still had to work on. There were documents to be copied, changes to be made, clarifications needed from the court. Filing the divorce with the court. One of these days.

It took me a couple of weeks to realize that he'd cleared all his stuff from the garage. All those beer boxes filled with God knows what, as well as his giant rolling tool chest and pottery wheel. And the raku kiln. He'd carted off the kiln! That heavy fucking lid I'd helped him lug across the yard. Oh, and the slab roller as well. All in the van? No, wait, there'd been a U-Haul parked in the vacant lot before he left. I'd even said something to him about it, wondering how long it would take one of the neighbors to call the cops because we'd had our share of itinerant squatters. (We'd never called the cops; in fact, Larry had let a homeless couple in a packing crate of a motor home help themselves to our electricity and water for a month). Larry said something like "fucking neighborhood busybodies," and I hadn't given the U-Haul another thought.

That Friday, with the sun barely above the horizon, I flew around the curve at El Morro cove, headed for work. I'd been sneaking in as early as possible as often as possible. Getting there in the dark seemed to make the day go faster. My job had just about run out, even though a lot of what I used to do kept creeping back—only now it was more difficult, because I had to consult online manuals to figure out how to do my old tasks the new way. The higher-ups had given me a multitude of odd jobs that made me feel like Nelson Mandela on Robben Island, carrying heavy rocks from one pile to another and then back again. A week earlier, I'd told the new guy in charge that if he saw a woman charging down the street screaming and ripping off her clothes, it would be me. He'd already grown used to my brand of humor, so he laughed. But I was half-serious. It would certainly shake things up.

And now, as I rounded the bend at El Morro, I was struck by the sight of a sailboat, a sliver of white suspended in a motionless, fog-shrouded continuum of sea and sky. A flock of pelicans hung in the air above. The sight was surreal, astonishing, heart-stopping. Without taking my eyes off the spectacle, I skidded onto the gravel and almost ran into a culvert on the side of the road. I sat staring at the scene for a long while, my body sliding down in the seat, my mind slowly unraveling. I thought about all the things I wanted to do with my life and how I wasn't doing any of them. How I was just going from one day to another, dealing with whatever life threw at me. Finally, as the faint orange sun rose, I eased back onto Pacific Coast Highway and drove on, slower than before.

I don't remember getting through the rest of the morning at work. Around midday, in the midst of stapling a report I'd finally managed to compile after slogging through one of the new computer programs—a monstrous tangle of postalese—I was seized by panic. I stood there, stapler and paper in hand. I felt like Alice in Wonderland, trapped, jammed halfway down the rabbit hole. I tried to take a breath. But I'd forgotten how. And then I was charging out of my office, through the lobby, and out onto the sidewalk. I stood there, blinking in the bright sunlight, and tried to breathe.

"Hey, you okay?" the receptionist called from the doorway.

I mumbled something about getting a cup of coffee and headed for Tully's in the little strip mall across the street. I ordered my "usual," a super dry cappuccino with two brown sugars, then plopped into the leather armchair near the door I'd always eyed but never stopped long enough to sit in. I rarely took lunch, figuring the time I spent rendering what my old boss used to call my "Psychotherapy Services" for the employees was my lunchtime. Today I was going to sit there as long as I felt like it. Maybe they'd fire me. I could only hope. I stared out across MacArthur Boulevard toward the toll road, a fast track home. I could be there in ten minutes. That's where I wanted to be. Right now. Worse than anything in the world. I wanted to move forward. It was only after the barista, a young college student and familiar face, walked over my cappuccino that I realized I hadn't paid him. He hadn't even reminded me. My wallet lay back at the office.

"Next time," he said with a grin. "Or not." And he headed back to the counter.

I stared at his back. Or not. As in, not ever having to return to this neighborhood? Well, I'd settle my bill, but that wasn't a bad idea. No more forcing myself to work at a job I hated. Truth was, now that I didn't have the expense of starting over, I could retire. So why was I still there? For a couple more dollars a month during retirement? Or was I afraid of being alone in the house every day? Could that be it? The idea pissed me off. I'd never had any trouble spending time alone. In fact I relished it, and I prided myself on that. But that was when I'd had a choice. I didn't have a choice now. If I was home, I would be alone. I stared out the window toward Laguna Beach. All I knew for sure was that I couldn't stuff myself back into that pinhole across the street. I sat there until I'd drained my cappuccino, and, with my heart doing loops in my chest, I made plans to retire. Maybe I'd also learn to paint a scene like the one I'd witnessed earlier that morning.

I told my boss the following day that I planned to retire, starting in two weeks. Due to the short notice, I expected problems. But it was almost a love-fest. We talked of life fully lived and better tomorrows. I floated, stumbled, soared, seized up, teared up, and hugged my way through those final days.

The morning after my last day at work, a Saturday, I awoke in a bubble that kept drifting up and up toward the ceiling with me inside. I stretched and yawned and fell back asleep. I didn't have to go anywhere. I didn't have to do anything. I could lie here all day long. I could eat artichokes at midnight for the rest of my life.

My indulgence lasted all of twenty minutes. Enough of that. There were things to do. I skipped downstairs. The first thing that leapt into view as I headed into the kitchen to make orange juice was the heap of divorce and trust papers. It hadn't gone away. I pinned it back onto my mental to-do list, made and drank my orange juice, fed Sweetpea and Jake, and headed for my closet to change for a hike. This was my day. This was my new life. The life I'd worked toward for thirty years. A part of me listened for the sound of silence, a forever-alone silence that I'd never pondered before.

"Wanna go for a walk?" I yelled to the dogs. They bounced, spun, and charged around, toenails clattering in the once-silent house.

Bending over to get a pair of shorts from the lower shelf of the Hobbit-sized closet where they were triple-folded to fit, I eased out the pair I wanted and then straightened. Why was I acting as if my soon-to-be ex-husband's T-shirts still hogged the shelf in their usual untidy sprawl? Hell, he'd already been gone for a month. Sliding the closet door wider, I scanned the shelves. I'd reorganize later. I was done living small, waiting for better days. I slipped on my shorts, pulled a sweatshirt over my head, and stopped. I couldn't wait. I had to start now. I started yanking out piles of clothing from the shelves. Jake and Sweetpea stared up at me expectantly. No hike?

"Sorry my loves, I'm on a mission—we'll go later, okay?"

But we didn't go later. We didn't go the following day, either; instead, I cleared out the closet, the one in the washroom, along with the shelves above the dryer and the drawers in the little room off the back door entrance. I forgot time, shifting from this area to that as an item of something or other led me to another task. By the time Sunday afternoon rolled around, stacks of clothing covered the floor in various rooms, along with shoes, towels, bedding, Christmas decorations, wrapping paper, photo albums, and a Goodwill pile consisting of clothes, shoes, and belts I hadn't worn in a while. And a pile for Larry: those car magazines that had arrived in the mail, a pair of bathing trunks, a couple of pairs of socks, and three antique baking soda tins I'd never liked. Each time I came across something of his, I got snagged on it for a moment, but it was never enough to stop me. Sweetpea and Jake settled onto whatever mound of clothing was closest to me, throwing anxious glances toward the door as if to remind me of my promise for a walk.

With darkness approaching, I switched on the light in my dressing room cum office where I'd started my campaign and glanced round at my handiwork, at all the rearranging that lay ahead of me. My gaze fell on a five-by-seven framed photo of me and Larry that sat on top of the filing cabinet next to the desk, which was also covered in photos. It was my favorite shot of us, of me, taken five years after we got married. My cousin—the same cousin who, along with her husband, hosted our first date that time in the Jacuzzi in Van Nuys when they first came to America—snapped it. We're sitting in their living room, Larry short-haired and trim-bearded, looking handsomely professorial, and me tanned and pensive with my hair, golden brown and long, piled on top of my head.

We'd gone up to Van Nuys to spend the weekend like we sometimes did. The second night, over a couple of bottles of wine (beer for Larry), we ended up talking about politics. My cousin's husband, a political junkie and shrewd businessman, was filled with facts and figures about the American system. Both he and my cousin loved Ronald Reagan. We didn't. I held my own with lots of exclaiming and gesticulating and more wine. Larry, as was his custom when it came to anything that smacked of contention, remained silent. At some point I appealed to him for backup on an opinion we both shared, something I knew he cared about. Elbows on the arms of his chair, he stared at me over the top of his fingers.

"Back me up here," I wailed.

Rolling his eyes, he spread out his hands, palms up, and shrugged.

I glared at him. "Just once. Just once, it would be nice if you actually—"

"Oh, leave him alone," my cousin's husband said with a twinkle in his eye. "He doesn't have to prove anything, he's got it all up here." He tapped his temple and grinned at Larry. "Haven't you?"

Larry let out an embarrassed laugh and squirmed around in his chair. "Oh yeah, I've got it all, all right."

My cousin's husband turned to me. "You'll never catch up to this guy, hey?"

I gave him a sour look. What was he up to? Without waiting for an answer, he launched into how every South African who comes to this country as an adult will always be about thirty to forty years behind Americans. We will never grow beyond our essential limitations because of the way we were raised, children barely seen and never heard, learning by rote and rulers across the knuckles, humiliated if we didn't follow the rules. And as a South African female, I was doubly screwed by the androcentric society, etc. Therefore, Larry would always be superior to me.

I laughed, one of those open-mouthed are-you-serious barks. I don't know what I said, but I felt slam-dunked by this man. And there was Larry, who I honestly expected to say something like, Oh, man, have you ever got that wrong. He'd never had a problem telling me how much he admired my smarts, my independent thinking. I really thought he'd stick up for me, present a united front. Make up for his former squirm-out. He didn't. Instead he grinned. At least he didn't lift his beer in a toast.

I picked up the photo. This definitely had to go too.

I glanced around at all the other framed photos in the room. It had been a big project for me, gathering snapshots of all "our" people: his kids and mine, our respective parents and grandparents. He'd barely glanced at any of them when I put them up, couldn't even tell which ones were his tribe and which were mine. It was hard to look at any of his immediate family now. They'd disappeared when Larry did. I wasn't going to take their abandonment personally—well, not too personally. Still, I didn't need a daily reminder of people who hadn't been there for me. I would give his family photos back to him, even though he hadn't bothered to take any of them himself besides a couple of Sweetpea and Jake.

As I reached for the shots of his grandparents from the wall, I stopped in front of the one of my dad sitting at a giant wooden desk the time he filled in for his boss at Nkana Main Shaft. A big old black-and-grey telephone sits on a metal cart behind him. The photo was taken six years after I emigrated to America, just before he died. White shirtsleeves rolled up to his elbows, a maroon, white, and navy-striped tie—one of the two he owned—loose around his neck, his arms resting atop a large desk calendar. There's a ballpoint pen in his right hand, as if he's about to write something. He was posing, I could tell. Tears filled my eyes. "I thought all men were true-blue like you," I said to the photo. "You ruined me with all your spoiling." He grinned back at me with that crooked, indulgent grin of his. And then I remembered what he'd scrawled on the back of the photo all those years ago: "Acting like I know what the hell I'm doing." I kissed the tip of my forefinger and touched the glass where his forehead was. "Me too, Dad. Me too."

Twenty-two

OVER THE NEXT two weeks, instead of rearranging all the stuff I'd thrown on the floor, I continued to sort through drawers and shelves. Working as if it were a full-time job, I rearranged my T-shirts, sweatshirts, shorts, and sweatpants into neat little stacks, piled most of my shoes into plastic boxes, and lined up the rest of them on newly purchased shelves. I had delivered most of my business blouses and skirts to Goodwill.

I entertained ideas about how to finish all those things Larry hadn't completed in the house after the various additions: caps for the toe-crippling edges of the dining room and bathroom floors, doors on the bathroom, a new closet in the washroom. Finally! And paint. Most of all, paint. The last time we'd painted the entire house was twenty-five years earlier, when we bought the place, although the additions had been painted after they were built. I had always wanted to complete these projects, but Larry's disinterest had derailed my plans. Why had I needed his enthusiasm? It was more than that, though—I'd needed his opinion, his concurrence.

I retrieved my ten-year-old ongoing file of plans to paint the house, swept aside the divorce and trust papers on the dining room table, and spread out the color sample cards and all those articles I'd collected on choosing paint colors: how to coordinate different shades throughout the house, what colors induced what moods, and information on the feng shui method—colors as a way to enhance and shift the flow of energy in your space. I flipped back and forth through the sample cards and color wheels. What went with what? Where to begin?

I looked around at the walls: "Navajo White"—wasn't that the name of the now-dingy off-white paint we'd used throughout the entire house? At the time the neutral shade was a good idea: it gave the Hobbit house an illusion of space, and I thought it would be the perfect canvas for our colorful, eclectic collection of paintings, ceramics, and blown-glass pieces. But now the color looked bleak, burdensome, and depressing. I just couldn't live with it anymore. I didn't have to.

Returning to my painting articles, my eye fell on a brochure: "Devine Color: The Wisdom of a Woman Inside Every Can. Follow the wisdom . . . trust the color." I grinned. Where on earth did this come from? I flipped the page and kept reading until this paragraph caught my eye. "The colors are truly trend-proof. So if you have a sofa from the '90s with a 200-year-old rug and a two-week-old kitchen remodel, you will find that not just one color but all the colors can coordinate everything and make it look 'meant to be.'"

I went online and found the Devine website. The company, headquartered in Oregon, had been conceived and was owned by a woman from Puerto Rico: "land of boundless color" is how she described her country. I loved the sound of that. The colors salsaed from the screen. I could taste them. I scrolled back and forth through the samples for hours. The following day I was at it again. But which of the colors went together, what about the feng shui aspect? I needed help. I called the phone number onscreen to set up a consultation.

A week later, Tara arrived with a suitcase filled with foldout sample books and nine-by-eleven color samples. She took a quick tour through the house, then suggested we sit on the floor in the dining room to work with the rich, buttery oak of the floors. This was to be the unifying color.

I couldn't sit still as she pulled out first one book then another, as well as the color samples, and spread them around her on the floor like a peacock's tail. Should I offer her a cup of tea? No. I couldn't wait to begin. She scrabbled through her briefcase. I stared at her. Had she forgotten a color swatch? One I might need? Giving a sigh of relief, she pulled out an unfurled color wheel, placed it in her lap, clasped her hands on top of it, and looked up at me. I realized I was nervous. What if I couldn't make up my mind? What if I hated the colors later? What if the rest of the world hated them? What if she favored Martha Stewart's subdued, middle-of-the-road colors? I didn't know it, but Tara had no intention of choosing the colors for me. She was there to find out what appealed to me and then to let me know what flowed.

"Okay, so what color strikes your fancy?" she asked brightly.

"Your shirt," I blurted. It was sage green. I loved the color.

Smiling, she fanned out the color wheel in her lap and pointed to a green. No, not quite it. More samples. I chose "Hosta," a deeper shade of green from the heart of the Amazon forest. More questions, more selections. I grew more confident with each color I selected. There was "Denim Blue"—essence of a hot African sky—and then "Ash," bottom-less and warm, and "Whip," a whisper of yellow, for balance. "Cocoa" was a bolt of inspiration that would cover one kitchen wall and one in my bedroom, "Mocha" a lighter shade for the kitchen cabinets. And then I found myself looking for an orangey red, something to shame an African sunset. My mother had once painted one of our walls at 24 Kantanta Street this color, just the one wall behind the dining room cum living room: "Terracotta," she called it. This complemented her furniture's autumn motif, as well as the white- and biscuit-colored doilies she'd crocheted for the side tables. It had been a bold strike on her part. Hardly anyone painted any of the mine houses themselves—and if they did it certainly wasn't with something as audacious as "Terracotta." Rhokana, the mining company, assumed responsibility for painting all the buildings in Nkana, and they always used white—or, in the case of public buildings, white and green. I suppose my mom wanted to make the house her own, different from all the other boxy, three- to four-bedroom brick houses.

I found the color I wanted. It was redder than my mom's "Terracotta." This one was "Cayenne." I had to have it. I would cover one living room wall with it like my mom had done. And how about the four walls of my dressing room/office? Too much? Out of control, out of flow? No, I wanted that balls-out color starting my day. It's what I felt inside, what I'd always felt inside, but it was an enthusiasm I had never felt confident expressing. But no more. This color represented the way in which I truly wanted to live my life.

To my surprise, Tara didn't even raise an eyebrow.

"It's you."

Going a little nutty, I chose "Shantung," a purple that made me want to dive naked into a vat filled with the stuff. It broke all the rules. From sunset-shaming red to flamboyant purple. I didn't care if Tara approved, if it flowed or not. I was following the Wisdom. Trusting the color. Trusting myself. From the corner of my eye I could see Tara flipping through her nine-by-eleven color samples, matching first one of the colors I'd chosen and then another to Shantung. She looked up and grinned.

"You've got some flow going on here."

It would take two months before I could get to the painting. First I had the floors redone and granite counters installed. This involved living with sheet-covered furniture and dunes of fine sawdust, and keeping Sweetpea and Jake from stomping across newly varnished floors. It was a good time to refinish the desk, butcher block, all the antique chairs, and the grandfather clock Larry's dad had built for us.

Ten days after Tara's visit I was walking down the road with Sweetpea and Jake when Larry called on my cell phone.

"Hey, are you still going to Darin's?"

His voice nailed me to the spot. My heart whacked against my ribcage. Sweetpea and Jake tugged me forward.

"Wait," I called to them, yanking on the leashes. Cell phone pressed between shoulder and ear, I undid the catches and sank down on a log in the vacant lot. The dogs wandered off.

"I'm not going anywhere—" he said through spotty reception.

"I'm talking to Sweets and Jake."

"How are they?"

"Fine," I said stiffly. I wanted to tell him not to come, that I'd found someone else to babysit Sweetpea and Jake. But I hadn't. I'd looked into specialized services that offered the kind of treatment Sweetpea needed, but I couldn't bear to traumatize her or leave either of them with a stranger. The logistics of it all were too overwhelming. I was stuck with Larry. For the time being.

"Listen," Larry said. "I can't talk for long, no reception—"

"Where are you?"

"What day do you leave?"

"Where are you?"

"Huh?"

His old trick of avoiding the question.

"May twenty-ninth."

"See you then," he said and hung up.

I glanced down at the telephone number: 541 area code. Oregon. The numbers blurred for a moment. That's where she lived. It was too much of a coincidence. I felt like one of those giant inflatable figures you see at auto dealerships—torso, head, and arms snapping in the breeze one moment, the next folded over, collapsing in on itself. I stood there, overwhelmed. But then suddenly I felt a surge of self-assurance, an inner strength that must have been building up these past two months. A vast quiet washed over me and I was filled with certainty. It didn't matter what he was doing.

He told me later that he'd wandered through New Mexico, Arizona, Nevada, and Northern California looking for a place to live, and then ended up in Oregon after that final escape. And looked her up. Just like that. Apparently she had a converted garage to rent and a couple of acres to tend. He told her he was going through a divorce because "things had gotten out of hand" back home.

He'd found a place to light. This was where he'd chosen to live. Later, the couple of times he came down to babysit the dogs, whenever I called Oregon his home he always said, "For now. Maybe I'll come home." My answer was always the same. Fuck no. I never knew whether he was serious or not. But it didn't matter. As for her—no, they weren't together. She was just a friend. He was living alone, just like he wanted to. Sometimes I believed him, sometimes I didn't.

I realized around this time that chunks of my accent had slipped back into their original baath and caan't pronunciations, part of the lexicon I'd tried to knead into the chocolaty American model upon arrival in the States. I'd never managed to lose my flat S'th Efrican plunk; however, time with Larry's drawl had done more to homogenize my enunciation than any of my conscious efforts had. That and his teasing. And now I found myself retreating to the accent that used to be so confusing to American ears.

I also started using the original name my mother had chosen for me when she was pregnant: Rossandra. It was the name of a sixteenth-century Portuguese galleon that appeared in an adventure novel she was reading at the time. In the book, the galleon is sailing up the west coast of Africa on a journey of exploration. The name never made it to my birth certificate; it was a little too long, a little too exotic. But it now felt right to me. I was definitely on a journey of exploration.

* * *

Ten days later, I jerked awake to the sound of the back door's squeak. I glanced at the clock: 12:40 a.m. My heart thudded.

"Woof, woof." A voice floated up the stairs.

For a moment I thought I was dreaming.

"Woof." This time in falsetto.

I tensed. Jake slowly rose onto his haunches and looked at me. Sweetpea stirred but snored on.

"Who's there?" I said in a hard voice. Jake's tail thumped.

"Great watchdogs," Larry called back. The light in the living room came on. Jake vibrated in place.

"Nice note."

"It was time to go." He appeared on the staircase. Sweetpea shot up and I grabbed her. In an excited state she was bound to do a header off the edge of the loft and onto the floor below. Nimble-footed Jake was off the bed before I could grab him; he threw himself against Larry as Larry reached the top step.

"Typical," I said. Sweetpea strained in my arms. "Better come say hi to her before she flips out."

Gently disengaging himself from Jake, Larry sat on the end of the bed. For the next couple of minutes, both dogs buried him with wriggles and licks until they had their fill and calmed down.

"How are you?" he said.

"Good, actually," I said.

He nodded and rose to his feet. "Well, I'd better let you get back to sleep, sorry I woke you."

"Night."

"Night." He eased back down the stairs, crab-like.

I fluffed up the pillow. Sweetpea and Jake circled, rearranged their portion of the bedclothes with a couple of scratches, adjusted their positions a few times, then settled down. The light went off downstairs and I lay there looking up at the ceiling in the faint light from the house across the street. I checked for the alien in my chest; it wasn't there. I wondered if something would hit me later. I grew drowsy.

"Can I come and sleep with you?" he called from downstairs.

My eyes popped open. "You mean sleep here. In this bed. Up here?"

"No, I mean sleep with you."

"Definitely not."

Silence.

"Good girl."

I grinned into the darkness. He just couldn't resist.

* * *

While I was visiting Darin and his family, Larry spoiled Sweetpea and Jake. He gave them more food than they were used to, including steak, which they were definitely not used to. He cleaned out the pond filter, trimmed the bamboo, did yard work, put more shiny parts onto the No-mad, and went surfing. He stayed for a couple of days after I returned from my visit to my son. And then left again while I was out getting my hair done—only this time he at least clued me in to when he "might" be leaving.

It was after this visit that he called from Willows, a little town along Interstate 5, above Sacramento. He was driving back to Oregon in the VW, now officially his.

"I miss you," he said.

A part of me leapt into the air, like Jake after his Frisbee, while the rest of me did a Sweetpea: ears pricked for a moment before flopping back down.

"I'm really a bad person, aren't I?" he continued when I didn't answer.

"No," I told him, and meant it. "You really aren't."

Twenty-three

IT WAS FINALLY time for the house to be painted. Two of my girl-friends from work, Linda and Brenda, came over early one Saturday morning and helped me remove everything from the walls and shelves, including that top ledge Larry and Layne added when they opened up the ceiling in the living room, right down to the Japanese netsuke on those two little shelves inches from the living room floor. We packed the smaller stuff into boxes and stashed the bigger items anywhere we could find space, including the top of the dining room table, burying the divorce and trust papers I had yet to complete.

That evening, grubby and exhausted, the three of us sat on the newly finished living room floor and celebrated with wine, bread, cheese, olives, chips and salsa, and some gooey dessert Brenda brought. We used one of the boxes as a table. We dissected my marriage for a bit.

"Here's to a whole new chapter," Brenda said, raising her glass in my direction.

Linda followed suit. "You've come a long way."

"Feels good," I said, clinking my glass against each of theirs. "Tender and new, but good."

Perhaps emboldened by their encouragement, after they left I headed for the dining room table, pulled out the divorce and trust package, and launched back into the almost completed documentation. Two days later after getting the clarifications I needed from the court and making copies, I mailed the divorce papers.

The painter I hired, a friend of a friend, took two months instead of the one he promised—plus he did shoddy work, leaving me with gaps that I'd spend months fixing. When he had removed all his cans, brushes, and drop cloths, I returned all the wall hangings and every piece of furniture to a new space on the wall or place on the floor. Thus rearranged, it was in the process of becoming my house.

* * *

On the day of our twenty-fifth wedding anniversary, I received a card from Larry. It was two months before our divorce was final. Standing on the back deck, I tore open the envelope and stood staring down at the anniversary card. The pond gurgled beside me. It was the first card I'd received from him for any occasion in ten years. It was oversized, the Taj Mahal of greetings cards, curlicued words screaming over a gold-ribboned spray of red roses: "On Our Special Anniversary With All My Love."

Was this some spontaneous purchase at the supermarket for its sheer sappiness? But why send me an anniversary card at all? Jake nudged his spit-soaked Frisbee up my ankle. Corny as it was, I would've gone mad over something like this at any other time in our marriage. But I didn't want it now. It blew me off course. I'd sorted through his "I've been thinking" comments, the ones about returning "home" during our phone conversations and those times he babysat the dogs. But this dug deeper. A lot deeper.

Jake groaned to remind me about the Frisbee and nudged it again. I threw it across the deck, then sank onto the doorstep and scanned the card's printed script. "Being married to you has been the best thing that's ever happened to me . . . my partner, my dearest friend . . . Knowing I have your love lets me face life's challenges . . . I love you with all my heart. Happy Anniversary." My heart thudded dully in my chest.

This was followed by Larry's handwritten message down at the bottom: "Here's the money I owe you, plus fifty dollars. Go out to dinner, maybe take a mannequin to sit with. Thinking of you. L."

Aah, this was more like it. This *had* been the supermarket find of the year. But why an anniversary card on the very day?

Sweetpea ambled over and sat on my foot. Slipping the card back into the envelope, I blocked out any further thoughts of it, kissed her between the eyes, then stood and threw the Frisbee a couple more times for Jake before heading into the house, where I slid the card face-down onto the top of the piano. For the most part I managed to dismiss the nature of the card and its timing. It was too crazy-making to consider.

A couple of days later, Larry called. I knew instantly that I hadn't been successful in dismissing the card. My heart jack-hammered in my chest, loud enough that I was sure he could hear it on the other end of the line. He called periodically, usually from the hill on the property next door where he sometimes took care of a couple of horses, a pig, and a donkey while the resident was away. It was the only place high enough to get cell phone reception. Larry with a cell phone: still a shocker. I almost hung up. Instead I kept my voice even as we exchanged pleasantries. He asked about the dogs and how I'd done installing the new pond pump.

We lapsed into our easy way of speaking to each other. I jokingly asked him if he'd already rustled up the "dogies" (motherless calves) for the day; he complained about the fucking snow while I gloated over the seventy-degree weather we were having; then I reminded him that he'd made his bed and now he had to lie in it. This had become my standard answer to any of his complaints about Oregon's Republican politics, the weather, the sometimes sheer starkness of where he lived. It gave me a small measure of satisfaction to do so. He always laughed and agreed.

"Oh, by the way, did you get my card?" he asked.

I didn't say anything for a moment. "Um, yes I did. Thanks?"

"You're welcome." Sweet. No inflection in his voice, no shiv up his sleeve; he missed the question in mine. Nothing more than you're welcome. I was thinking of you on our day. I do still love you, you know that, don't you? Got a kick out of the card, did you get it? Done deal.

But it wasn't a done deal for me. A vault buried deep within my heart had cracked open, sending tendrils of hope snaking through my chest, up my jaw, and down my arms, filling me with a sweet tenderness for all the good that had been between us. But then I heard the silence stretch on the other end of the line. Oh my God. I was waiting for him to Come Forward! I was waiting for him to say that in his time away he'd finally figured everything out and he'd realized what he was missing. He was tired of running away and he'd do anything to get back on track with me. But even as I waited, I knew it was too late. I relaxed my grip on the phone. These were only echoes of old dreams. We had a history together, and I still loved him. I would always love him. But I also knew nothing had changed. That it could never change enough for me. I wanted so much more from life. I wanted to move forward. What it came down to was him or me. And I chose me.

We said good-bye and I hung up. It would take me another three months to retrieve the card from where it lay on the piano and tuck it into the back of one of my new photo boxes, the one filled with old family photos.

Our divorce was finalized on May 13, 2008.

* * *

I returned to South Africa the following December for two weeks. Layne and Irma's house was complete: two stories of concrete and glass and a pool the length of the house in one of those new developments mushrooming all over the Johannesburg and Pretoria area. I received the same star treatment at the airport as before, with Layne, Irma, Illanka, Bianca, and Daegan all giving me body-crushing hugs. Glorious!

The first night Irma and I talked until midnight. This became a habit. She'd quit her job and was considering starting her own financial consulting business. She'd had it with South Africa's glass ceiling for women in management. Layne spent almost all his free time with me. We would follow each other from room to room and share trips in the car with the whole family.

As this was Christmas "hols," as they say, Daegan was bored. All his friends were back in Nelspruit, or at the coast. So other than Bianca's boyfriend or Layne, it was me who jumped off the second-story balcony and into the pool below with him or played this game where you had to dive for "treasure." We also spent time writing together—me with my memoir on Irma's laptop, him the life story of his rugby hero on his dad's computer.

A couple of days later, Garth flew over from Durban to spend a week with us. Sheila drove him to the airport, and then the airlines provided a wheelchair and whatever assistance he needed. I don't know what I expected, but the sight of him dragging his right leg, right hand curled close to his body while he shoved along a three-pronged cane with his left hand, made me want to drop to my knees and wail. Instead, I took a deep breath and wrapped my arms around his bird body, cane and all. He slid his good arm around my shoulder and we just stood there. It seemed he might've stayed there all day and all night if I hadn't finally drawn back. He told me he'd had a stroke and that he was coming along nicely, except he'd been constipated lately.

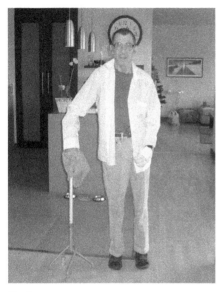

Garth

Dinner that first night with him was a meal from my childhood: pork roast with crackling, gem squash, and mashed potatoes and gravy. And like when we were children, Garth ate only the meat.

"You should eat your vegetables," I told him.

"Ja."

"Seriously, that's why you're constipated."

He smiled and continued to cut his meat into tiny pieces and chew with dentures that clattered. He spent most of his time watching TV; here, unlike at home, he had the remote. Sunny, the Ndebele maid—almost everyone still has a maid in South Africa, except they are now unionized—made Garth's morning tea and his breakfast: porridge with a dab of butter and sugar. I made his lunch, a cold meat sandwich. A couple of nights he had a beer before going to bed around eight. It was on one of those nights I asked him if Dad ever drank beer. It struck me that this was something I should've remembered about him.

"Ja," he said, "Dad sometimes had a Castle, but he liked his Royal more."

"What's that?"

"Wine. Red."

"How about that? I just remember them drinking gin and stuff like that."

"Mom liked her vodka."

"No shit."

"I used to drink vodka."

I gaped at him.

"But it's not good for you," he continued.

"You're quite the treasure trove of the past, aren't you?"

He looked uncertain for a moment, then nodded.

I was worried about how Garth was going to make it up the two flights of stairs to the bedroom Daegan had given up for him. It was next to my "suite," the one that was supposed to lure me back to South Africa. All the bedrooms were on the second floor. This was one of the reasons why Garth hadn't moved in with them. So here we were on the first night, Layne and Daegan dropping the girls off somewhere, Irma on her exercise machine in her bedroom. I was outside on the patio next to the pool, writing. Garth had been glued to the TV, but now from the corner of my eye I saw him at the foot of the stairs, his cane on the first step. The steel and wire banister was on the right—his bad side.

"Hey," I said, jumping up. "Why didn't you tell me you wanted to go to bed?"

"It's my bedtime." Bad hand pinned to his chest, he put his good foot on the first step and tried to place his cane on the next with his left hand, but couldn't reach that high.

"Here, let me help you."

Ignoring me, he angled his cane this way and that until it landed where he wanted. I cupped his elbow and lifted him and the cane to the next step. We bumbled up the next couple of steps; he kept trying to do it by himself.

"Here, let me carry you," I said.

Nudging up eyeglasses half the size of his face, he handed me his cane, twisted around, and pulled himself up the banister with his left hand, sliding his bad foot onto the next step. After a while he made it all the way to the top by himself with me below, ready to catch him.

"Mannn," I said at the top. "You bloody well did it, didn't you?"

He gave me a shy smile and took the cane from me.

"Listen," I said, "you must wake me in the morning. Getting down-stairs is a whole other proposition, okay?"

"All right." He shuffled to Daegan's bedroom. In the morning he was already downstairs before I got there. He fell only once, he told me.

Sunny approached me on the second day of Garth's visit. With her hand over her heart she drew me close. "Your brother, he is all right?"

"Ja, nee," I said. Yes, no: a typical South African expression.

"And you live in America?"

The question jammed a thumb into a tender muscle. I nodded.

"It is far, far way."

I nodded again.

"It is nice there, hey?"

"I like it very much."

She thought about it for a moment, then said, "Your son, he is here. That is good. I will pray for your brother."

The following October, Garth and Margaret moved into Shepstone Place, "Home for the Aged" in Escourt, about 290 miles from Layne. It's an old brick building that resembles a colonial hospital, right down to the red polished floors and the tea trolleys that roll up and down the halls for morning and afternoon tea. Its thick green lawns and tree- and flower-covered grounds are manned by an army of khaki-clad Africans.

Their room is small but perfect for "two old cripples," as Garth matter-of-factly noted. His hearing has gotten so bad that I'm back to writing letters and sending cards. He's asked me to start addressing him as Mac, the name our father went by.

* * *

Shortly after I returned from South Africa, I stopped at NurseryLand and bought a black wrought iron bistro set, two chairs and a table with inset gold-, brown-, and fawn-colored ceramic tiles arranged in a wheel design. I'd always wanted one. Larry thought them "dumb"—I could never get him tell me why, but it was enough to make me give up on the idea. But now there was no one and nothing to discourage me from getting it. For the first week I ate breakfast, lunch, and dinner at my bistro set, no matter the weather. If it was cold I'd wrap myself in a warm blanket as protection from the damp cold of the canyon.

Sometimes Sweetpea sat opposite me in the other chair, butt sideways, constantly having to shift her paws to stay put on the small round metal seat. She and Jake had worked it out; he never once tried to sit there, not even if she wasn't around. Every now and then she did her little throat-clearing thing and stared off into whatever direction she happened to be facing at the time. Whenever I spoke to her she would turn, ears fully pricked, white-rimmed eyes boring into mine. I'd say something like "I love you" or "You're so beautiful" and her ears would relax—if she were human I could go ahead and tell you that her face would soften, her eyes would crinkle at the edges, and she would give me a look as intimate as any I've ever shared with anyone.

Epilogue

ELEVEN MONTHS AFTER our divorce became final, Sweetpea died. Not from the failure of her damaged kidney—she died from cancer of the spleen, which spread to her liver before we caught it.

I don't remember leaving the building after Dr. Donner told me that Sweetpea's kidney function was doing quite well, as it had been for some time, but that she'd developed cancer of the spleen and possibly the liver. I do remember Sweetpea doing her usual routine, grinning and wiggling at every human in sight as we headed down the hallway and out the building, albeit a little slower than during her last visit. She was a popular girl—always so cooperative, despite what they had to do to conduct their tests. I'd always envisioned The Back Room as this chamber of horrors, dogs strapped down with plastic tubes poking out. Her framed black-and-white eight-by-ten photo hung down the hall from the examination room we usually used. It probably still does. I'd visited her photo minutes before the diagnosis, giving my usual appreciation and thanks to All That Is for the wonder that was Sweetpea and for the time I'd had with her. And I begged for her to live longer than any normal dog.

After the diagnosis, I thought back to that first day we brought her into the Center as a six-month-old with a death sentence, how I'd prayed for just one year of life for her. She'd made it seven years and four months. Not nearly long enough.

Somehow I made it to the car. Sweetpea jumped onto the passenger seat, settled back and stared straight ahead, ready to roll. I leaned over and fell on her neck, sobbing. Struggling for breath, she lifted her head and licked my forehead, an apologetic expression on her face.

"Sorry, baby girl," I said. I sat up and grabbed a wad of tissues from the box on the floor on the passenger side, emptying it. She did her little throat-clearing thing and pawed the air for scratches. Rubbing her ear and shoulder with one hand, I dialed Larry's number on my cell phone with the other. I had to share the burden of this terrible news; I had to feel better. Besides, he would want to know. After misdialing twice, I got through.

"She only has a couple of weeks," I wailed.

"Wha—"

"Sweetpea."

"Oh God," he said. He sounded far away. There was a long silence. "Are you there?"

"Yeah," he finally said, his voice choked with tears. All those years I'd wondered if Sweetpea would be the one to get through to him. "I've been dreading this moment."

"I know," I whispered. "Me too."

"I'll leave as soon as I can."

He arrived the following afternoon. I was in the kitchen making tea. He made straight for Sweetpea the moment he walked in the door. She lay in her donut bed, front legs folded beneath her, nose buried in the side. Without lifting her head, she crinkled her eyes at him and shifted around. He fell to his knees, kissed the top of her head, and then lay beside her on the floor. "Oh, baby girl," he whispered. At some point he got up and hugged me.

Sweetpea hung on for the next five weeks. She stopped eating for the most part; I couldn't get her to take her pills, and she was always so tired. Still, she managed to give me that lift of the chin that said, Hey, baby, you're my human. She continued to cling to me in our queen-sized bed, head on her own pillow, so close a flea couldn't turn around between us. Right up until the last night of her life, when she was sneezing blood, she awoke a couple of times as usual to paw the air for scratches and kisses.

I spent every available moment with Sweetpea. Two thoughts played on an endless loop in my mind: I don't want to miss one single second with you, and I want to fill myself with future memories of you. Over and over again, I kissed the broad space between her eyes, her stomach, the downy-like spot behind her ears, the tops of her paws—a favorite of mine for the pure sweet smell of her dogginess.

During this time, Larry never left the house. It was understood that he would stay until the end. He slept on an air mattress on the living room floor, watching TV late into the night. We didn't talk much. Most of the time he sat on the couch watching his old Westerns with Sweetpea at his side, his arm around her, Jake always close by. We shared the stressful, heartbreaking task of trying to get her to take her pills. If she'd just take the pills she'd make it, I told myself. I kept believing there would be some miraculous recovery, and continued to stuff the cut-up pills in food like I'd always done: cheese, bacon, Greenies, beetroot—a favorite of hers—but now she also got salmon, steak, and cookies. She'd take a

Sweetpea's Grave Marker

nibble as if to please me, then she'd press her nose back into the side of her bed, look up at me with those white-rimmed Staffie eyes, and sigh.

I anguished over whether I was being fair to her by keeping her alive. Spleen cancer isn't painful, the vet said. You will know when it's time, he told me. I didn't know. All I knew was that I didn't want her to die. I probably let her hang on too long. Larry was his usual deferring self. It was up to me. When her dime-sized shits were the product of a five-minute strain, I knew I had to call it. The day before the vet was to come to the house to help her on her way, she ambled out the front gate that I'd left open and sat in the driveway in that sideways way of hers. She craned her neck around the bamboo, looking up and then down the street in search of somebody to greet.

On April 20, 2009, Sweetpea dragged herself from her donut bed under my desk and offered Dr. G and his assistant as full a body wiggle as she could manage, and then they did the deed. I stroked and kissed her until the light went out of her eyes.

After the two men left, Larry came from the side of the house. He looked at Sweetpea's body and, with one hand on the bookcase for support, hunched over, head hanging. His body shuddered with deep, heaving sobs. He didn't bother to stem the flow of tears with his other hand; it just hung by his side. It was like sixty years of tears from all those feelings bound up inside him had finally found an outlet. I rose to my feet and walked over to him. He enveloped me in a long, swaying, tight, wet hug and continued to cry unashamedly.

* * *

We buried her in the front yard against the fence between the upright railroad tie—the one with my ceramic elf man—and the bougainvillea, along with Larry's favorite surf fin and a sweet-faced little angel statue a friend gave me. Grey-faced, he dug the grave. It was his idea to wrap her in the new leather lumberjack-type jacket he'd bought in Oregon just months before. We played Warren Zevon's "Knocking on Heaven's Door" from the album Zevon made just before he died of cancer.

Jake had this incredulous expression on his face when Larry started tossing shovelfuls of dirt over Sweetpea's body. His gaze bounced from me to Larry to the grave then back again. "You're making a mistake," his desperate look said. He kept nudging the dirt away with his nose. For a long time afterward he would amble over to the grave, sniff around, look from left to right, and then pee against the upright railroad tie.

Larry built this six-foot-high upside down L-shaped wooden contraption so we could hang a plant over the grave. On the side of one of the boards, he printed with a fine brush in red paint: "Sweetpea White—Our Baby Girl, 2001-2009."

I hung a fern above the grave and planted Australian violets on top—a ground cover with tiny bouquets of mauve, white-tipped flowers. Nothing had ever grown in that space before, not even weeds. I was desperate that these violets would grow. I wanted them to take over the yard, then the canyon, then Laguna Beach. I consulted with my gardening buddy on how to do just that.

"No problem," she said. "They'll take off, you just wait and see."

For the next two months I took daily walks in the hills with Jake. I rediscovered my neighborhood and all the people I'd always raced past, iPod buds in my ears. And then one night, after a toilet break around midnight, I found myself standing outside on the front deck beside my sweet little bistro set. Ever since the divorce, part of me had been dreading a moment like this, a middle-of-the-night terror. After all the busyness and the worry over Sweetpea had stopped, I would finally be forced to admit that I was well and truly alone. So here I stood, naked—pajamas were only for when guests came—and shivering a little. Summer was coming soon. The moon was so bright I could've read the bottom line of an eye chart. The air was still and cool.

Jake ambled from the house and peed against the bistro table leg and then, like the good companion he is, settled an inch from my foot. He glanced up at me, and then at Sweetpea's grave. The plants had thrived, just like my plant buddy had promised. In the radiance of the moon, the white tips of the violets shimmered and danced across the grave before streaming around the railroad tie and into the gaps left by the blight that had attacked the bamboo in front of my writing studio. Tears filled my eyes.

"Look at your flowers, baby girl," I whispered, and waited for a storm of self-pity and loneliness to hit me. Instead, all I felt was the pure, clean pain of loss for my beloved dog and a deep sadness for Larry and for what might've been between us. But nothing more. I sank down onto the bistro chair and sobbed until I couldn't cry any more. This was the first time I'd cried over the loss of my marriage since the day he left for the last time. I'd been too afraid to cry. Afraid that mourning the loss would take me back to a time when I didn't trust myself. Now the cry felt good and honest and cleansing.

Distressed by my sobs, Jake disappeared, only to return a few moments later with his Frisbee, which he dropped beside my foot. I spent the next ten minutes throwing it across the deck for him and admiring Sweetpea's flowers before we turned in for the night.

Jake and His Frisbee

the end

Acknowledgments

I'D LIKE TO THANK Jeanne Smith, who read all my shitty drafts, always available, always encouraging, always brutally honest. And very special thanks to my dog, Jake, without whom this book couldn't have been finished.

About the author

ROSSANDRA WHITE, secure in marriage to the American man of her dreams and working for the Postal Service in administration, took up writing to quiet the voices from the past back home in Africa. The result: *Monkey's Wedding* and *Mine Dances*, two young adult novels about family, race, and the dark magic of a society poised on the brink of change. And then her world fell apart when her marriage unraveled, along with a crisis back home in Africa and the worsening ill health of her beloved dog. *Loveyoubye*, her memoir, resulted as a way to heal the past and to face the future. She lives in Laguna Beach, California with her two Staffordshire Bull Terriers with whom she fights for space in her bed. When she's not writing, she enjoys yoga, Jazzercize, and hiking the hills behind her home in Laguna canyon.

SELECTED TITLES FROM SHE WRITES PRESS

She Writes Press is an independent publishing company founded to serve women writers everywhere. Visit us at www.shewritespress.com.

Letting Go into Perfect Love: Discovering the Extraordinary After Abuse by Gwendolyn M. Plano. $16.95, 978-1-938314-74-2. After staying in an abusive marriage for twenty-five years, Gwen Plano finally broke free—and started down the long road toward healing.

Seeing Red: A Woman's Quest for Truth, Power, and the Sacred by Lone Morch. $16.95, 978-1-938314-12-4. One woman's journey over inner and outer mountains—a quest that takes her to the holy Mt. Kailas in Tibet, through a seven-year marriage, and into the arms of the fierce goddess Kali, where she discovers her powerful, feminine self.

Splitting the Difference: A Heart-Shaped Memoir by Tré Miller-Rodríguez. $19.95, 978-1-938314-20-9. When 34-year-old Tré Miller-Rodríguez's husband dies suddenly from a heart attack, her grief sends her on an unexpected journey that culminates in a reunion with the biological daughter she gave up at 18.

Don't Call Me Mother: A Daughter's Journey from Abandonment to Forgiveness by Linda Joy Myers. $16.95, 978-1-938314-02 -5. Linda Joy Myers's story of how she transcended the prisons of her childhood by seeking—and offering—forgiveness for her family's sins.

Americashire:A Field Guide to a Marriage by Jennifer Richardson. $15.95, 978-1-938314-30-8. A couple's decision about whether or not to have a child plays out against the backdrop of their new home in the English countryside.

Warrior Mother: A Memoir of Fierce Love, Unbearable Loss, and Rituals that Heal by Sheila K. Collins, PhD. $16.95, 978-1-938314-46-9. The story of the lengths one mother goes to when two of her three adult children are diagnosed with potentially terminal diseases.